Windows 11
Frequently Asked Questions

2024 Edition

Kevin Wilson

Elluminet Press

www.elluminetpress.com

Windows 11 FAQ: 2024 Edition

Publisher: Elluminet Press
Director: Kevin Wilson
Lead Editor: Steven Ashmore
Technical Reviewer: Mike Taylor, Robert Ashcroft
Copy Editors: Joanne Taylor, James Marsh
Proof Reader: Mike Taylor
Indexer: James Marsh
Cover Designer: Kevin Wilson

eBook versions and licenses are also available for most titles. Any source code or other supplementary materials referenced by the author in this text is available to readers at www.elluminetpress.com/resources

For detailed information about how to locate your book's resources, go to www.elluminetpress.com/resources

Table of Contents

About the Author

With over 20 years' experience in the computer industry, Kevin Wilson has made a career out of technology and showing others how to use it. After earning a master's degree in computer science, software engineering, and multimedia systems, Kevin has held various positions in the IT industry including graphic & web design, programming, building & managing corporate networks, and IT support.

He serves as senior writer and director at Elluminet Press Ltd, he periodically teaches computer science at college, and works as an IT trainer in England while researching for his PhD. His books have become a valuable resource among the students in England, South Africa, Canada, and in the United States.

Kevin's motto is clear: "If you can't explain something simply, then you haven't understood it well enough." To that end, he has created the Exploring Tech Computing series, in which he breaks down complex technological subjects into smaller, easy-to-follow steps that students and ordinary computer users can put into practice.

Acknowledgements

Thanks to all the staff at Luminescent Media & Elluminet Press for their passion, dedication and hard work in the preparation and production of this book.

To all my friends and family for their continued support and encouragement in all my writing projects.

To all my colleagues, students and testers who took the time to test procedures and offer feedback on the book

Finally thanks to you the reader for choosing this book. I hope it helps you to use your computer with greater understanding.

Have fun!

1

User Interface & Navigation

How do I use virtual desktops in Windows 11?

How do I use the Snap Layouts feature in Windows 11?

How do I use File Explorer in Windows 11?

How do I use the new Quick Settings?

How do I use touchpad gestures in Windows 11?

How do I search for files and apps in Windows 11?

How do I set up multiple monitors in Windows 11?

How do I create custom keyboard shortcut?

How do I pin websites to the taskbar in Windows 11?

How do I navigate using keyboard shortcuts?

How Do I Adjust Volume in Windows 11?

How Do I Adjust Screen Brightness in Windows 11?

Chapter 1: User Interface & Navigation

How do I use virtual desktops in Windows 11?

Virtual desktops allow you to organize your workspace by creating multiple desktop environments. This can help you separate different tasks, such as work, personal use, gaming, or studying, making your workflow more efficient and less cluttered.

1. Accessing Virtual Desktops

Using the Task View Button:

- **Task View Button:** Located on the taskbar (usually to the right of the Start button), the Task View button looks like two overlapping rectangles. Clicking it will open the Task View interface, displaying all your current virtual desktops and open windows.

Using Keyboard Shortcuts:

- **Open Task View:** Press Win + Tab to open the Task View directly.

2. Creating a New Virtual Desktop

Via Task View:

1. Open Task View by clicking the Task View button or pressing Win + Tab.

2. At the top of the screen, click on the **"New desktop"** button (a + icon).

3. A new virtual desktop will be created, and you can switch to it immediately.

Using Keyboard Shortcut:

- Press Win + Ctrl + D to create a new virtual desktop instantly and switch to it.

3. Switching Between Virtual Desktops

Using Task View:

1. Open Task View (Win + Tab).

2. Click on the virtual desktop you want to switch to.

Using Keyboard Shortcuts:

- **Switch to Next Desktop:** Press Win + Ctrl + Right Arrow.

- **Switch to Previous Desktop:** Press Win + Ctrl + Left Arrow.

Using Touchpad Gestures (on supported devices):

- Swipe three or four fingers to the left or right on your touchpad to switch between desktops.

4. Managing Open Windows Across Desktops

Moving Windows to Another Desktop:

1. Open Task View (Win + Tab).

2. Right-click on the window you want to move.

3. Hover over **"Move to"** and select the desired virtual desktop or choose **"New desktop"** to create a new one.

Dragging Windows Between Desktops:

- In Task View, click and drag a window thumbnail from one desktop to another.

5. Closing a Virtual Desktop

Via Task View:

1. Open Task View (Win + Tab).

2. Hover over the virtual desktop you want to close.

3. Click the **"X"** button that appears in the top-right corner of the desktop thumbnail.

Using Keyboard Shortcut:

- Press Win + Ctrl + F4 while on the virtual desktop you wish to close.

Note: When you close a virtual desktop, any open windows on that desktop will move to the previous desktop.

6. Renaming Virtual Desktops

Naming your virtual desktops can help you keep them organized.

Steps to Rename:

1. Open Task View (Win + Tab).

2. Right-click on the virtual desktop you want to rename.

3. Select **"Rename"** from the context menu.

4. Enter the desired name and press Enter.

7. Customizing Virtual Desktops

Each virtual desktop can have its own background wallpaper, allowing for visual differentiation.

Changing the Background for a Specific Desktop:

1. Switch to the virtual desktop you want to customize.

2. Right-click on the desktop and select **"Personalize"**.

3. Choose a new background image from the available options or browse your files.

4. The new background will apply only to the current virtual desktop.

8. Tips and Best Practices

- **Use Virtual Desktops for Different Purposes:** For example, dedicate one desktop for work-related applications, another for personal browsing and media, and another for gaming or creative projects.

- **Keyboard Shortcuts Are Your Friend:** Familiarize yourself with keyboard shortcuts to navigate and manage virtual desktops more efficiently.

- **Organize Open Windows:** Keep similar applications grouped together on the same virtual desktop to maintain an organized workspace.

- **Remember Resource Usage:** While virtual desktops help with organization, having too many open desktops with numerous applications can consume more system resources.

How do I use the Snap Layouts feature in Windows 11?

Snap Layouts in Windows 11 are an enhanced window management feature that allows you to quickly organize and arrange your open applications on your screen. By providing predefined layout options, Snap Layouts help you maximize productivity and maintain an organized workspace with minimal effort.

1. Accessing Snap Layouts

There are multiple ways to access Snap Layouts in Windows 11:

A. Using the Mouse

- **Hover Over the Maximize Button:**

  o Move your cursor to the **maximize** button (the square icon) in the top-right corner of any window.

  o After a brief moment, a small popup will appear,

displaying various layout options.

- **Select a Layout:**

  o Click on one of the highlighted areas within the layout to snap the current window into that position.

  o The remaining areas will highlight, allowing you to select other open windows to fill those spaces.

B. Using Keyboard Shortcuts

- **Snap Using Arrow Keys:**

  o **Win + Z:** Opens the Snap Layouts menu for the active window.

  o Alternatively, use **Win + Arrow Keys** to snap windows:

    - **Win + Left Arrow:** Snap the window to the left half of the screen.

    - **Win + Right Arrow:** Snap the window to the right half.

    - **Win + Up Arrow:** Maximize the window or snap to the top half.

    - **Win + Down Arrow:** Minimize or snap to the bottom half.

- **Navigate Layouts:**

  o After pressing **Win + Z**, use the arrow keys to choose a layout and press **Enter** to select.

C. Using Touch Gestures (For Touchscreen Devices)

- **Drag the Window:**

  o Touch and hold the window's title bar, then drag it to the desired edge or corner of the screen.

  o Release to snap the window into place, and similar to mouse usage, select other windows to fill the remaining spaces.

2. Using Snap Layouts with the Mouse

- **Open Multiple Windows:**

- o Ensure you have multiple application windows open that you want to arrange.

- **Access Snap Layouts:**

  - o Hover your cursor over the maximize button of the window you want to snap.

- **Choose a Layout:**

  - o A popup with various layout options (e.g., two columns, three columns, grid) will appear.

  - o Click on the desired section within the layout to snap the window accordingly.

- **Fill Remaining Spaces:**

  - o After snapping the first window, the other open windows will display as thumbnails in the remaining sections.

  - o Click on each thumbnail to snap them into the designated spaces.

Example: Two-Column Layout. Snap one window to the left half and another to the right half.

3. Using Snap Layouts with Keyboard Shortcuts

For users who prefer keyboard navigation, Snap Layouts can be efficiently managed using shortcuts:

Chapter 1: User Interface & Navigation

- **Activate Snap Layouts:**

  o Press **Win + Z** to open the Snap Layouts menu for the active window.

- **Select a Layout:**

  o Use the arrow keys to navigate through the available layouts.

  o Press **Enter** to select the desired layout.

- **Assign Windows to Layout Sections:**

  o After selecting the layout, Windows will prompt you to choose other open windows to fill the remaining sections.

  o Navigate to the desired window using the arrow keys and press **Enter** to assign.

Additional Shortcuts:

- **Win + Left/Right Arrow:** Quickly snap windows to the left or right half without opening the Snap Layouts menu.

- **Win + Shift + Left/Right Arrow:** Move the snapped window to a different monitor in a multi-monitor setup.

4. Managing Snapped Windows

Once you've arranged your windows using Snap Layouts, managing them becomes straightforward:

A. Resizing Snapped Windows

- **Adjust Divider:**

  o Hover your cursor over the border between two snapped windows until it changes to a resize cursor.

  o Click and drag to adjust the size of the windows proportionally.

B. Moving Windows Between Sections

- **Drag and Drop:**

  o Click and hold the title bar of a snapped window.

  o Drag it to a different section of the Snap Layout to move it.

- **Use Keyboard Shortcuts:**

  o Select the window and use **Win + Arrow Keys** to snap it to a different position.

C. Closing Snapped Windows

- **Close Individually:**

  o Close each window as you normally would, using the close button (**X**) or keyboard shortcut (**Alt + F4**).

- **Close Entire Layout:**

  o If you want to exit the Snap Layout entirely, you can maximize one of the snapped windows, which will return it to full-screen and release the others.

How do I use File Explorer in Windows 11?

File Explorer in Windows 11 serves as the primary tool for navigating, managing, and organizing your files and folders.

1. Open File Explorer by pressing **Win + E** or clicking the folder icon pinned to the taskbar by default.

Chapter 1: User Interface & Navigation

2. Explore the **new tabs feature** by clicking the + icon at the top of File Explorer. This allows you to open multiple tabs within one window for easier multitasking.

3. Pin frequently used folders to Quick Access by right-clicking on them then selecting **Pin to Quick access**. These pinned items will appear in the left sidebar under Quick Access.

4. Once File Explorer is open, familiarize yourself with its key components:

   - **Simplified Toolbar:**
     - ☐ Located at the top, it includes essential actions such as **New**, **Cut**, **Copy**, **Paste**, **Delete**, **Rename**, and **Properties**.

   - **Navigation Pane:**
     - ☐ On the left side, it provides quick access to locations like **Quick Access**, **This PC**, **Network**, and connected drives.
     - ☐ **Quick Access** displays frequently used folders and recently accessed files for easy retrieval.

   - **Address Bar:**
     - ☐ Shows the current folder path.
     - ☐ Click on any part of the path to navigate to that directory.
     - ☐ You can also type directly into the address bar to jump to a specific location.

   - **Main Pane:**
     - ☐ Displays the contents of the selected folder, including files and subfolders.
     - ☐ You can interact with items here by double-clicking, right-clicking, or using keyboard shortcuts.

   - **Preview and Details Panes:**
     - ☐ **Preview Pane:** Shows a preview of the selected file (e.g., image, document).
       - ☐ Toggle by clicking the **Preview** icon in the toolbar.

☐ **Details Pane:** Provides detailed information about the selected file, such as size, type, and date modified.

    ☐ Toggle by clicking the **Details** icon in the toolbar.

• **Status Bar:**

    ☐ Located at the bottom, it displays information about the selected items, like file size and the number of items.

5. Customize folder layouts, select a folder, then click **View** on the toolbar. Select from options like:

    o **Details** to view file information such as size and date.

    o **Large/Extra Large icons** for a visually rich display. Useful for folders that contain videos and images.

6. Search for specific files using the search bar at the top-right corner of the window. Enter keywords and refine results by selecting filters like **Date modified**, **File type**, or **Size**.

How do I use the new Action Center (Quick Settings)?

1. Open the Quick Settings by pressing **Win + A** or clicking the area near the clock on the taskbar.

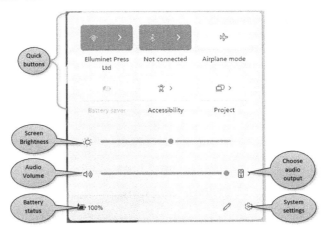

2. Edit Quick Settings by clicking the **pencil icon** in the bottom-right corner of the Quick Settings panel. Drag tiles like Wi-Fi, Bluetooth, or Battery Saver to rearrange them or click **Add** to include additional options.

3. Use the **Volume** and **Brightness** sliders within the panel to quickly adjust these settings.

4. Toggle settings such as **Airplane Mode**, **Night Light**, or **Focus Assist** by clicking their respective icons.

5. Scroll up in the Quick Settings to view grouped notifications. Dismiss individual notifications by clicking the **X** next to them or click **Clear all** to remove all notifications.

How do I use touchpad gestures in Windows 11?

Optimizing touchpad settings can enhance your navigation experience on laptops.

1. **Open Touchpad Settings:**

   o Press **Windows key + I** to open Settings App.

   o Navigate to **Bluetooth & devices > Touchpad**.

2. **Adjust Touchpad Sensitivity:**

   o In the Touchpad settings, find the **Touchpad sensitivity** dropdown.

   o Choose from options like **Most sensitive**, **High sensitivity**, **Medium sensitivity**, or **Low sensitivity** based on your preference.

3. **Configure Taps:**

   o Enable or disable **Tap to click** by toggling the switch.

   o Adjust **Tap pressure** if available, to set how hard you need to tap the touchpad.

4. **Set Up Gestures:**

   o **Three-finger gestures:**

   ▪ **Swipe up:** Open Task View.

   ▪ **Swipe down:** Show desktop.

   ▪ **Swipe left or right:** Switch between open apps.

   ▪ **Tap:** Assign a custom action or open a specific app.

   o **Four-finger gestures:** (if supported)

- Customize actions like opening specific virtual desktops or launching particular apps.

5. **Scrolling and Zooming:**

   o Enable **Two-finger scrolling** for vertical and horizontal navigation.

   o Enable **Pinch to zoom** for zooming in and out within apps.

6. **Advanced Settings:**

   o Click on **Advanced gestures** to explore more customization options.

   o Adjust settings for specific gestures like **Drag two fingers to scroll** or **Rotate with two fingers**.

7. **Enable or Disable Touchpad:**

   o If you need to disable the touchpad temporarily, toggle the **Touchpad** switch to **Off**.

Tips:

- Experiment with different sensitivity levels and gestures to find the setup that best suits your workflow.

- If your laptop supports it, update touchpad drivers through **Device Manager** or the manufacturer's website for improved performance and additional features.

How do I search for files and apps in Windows 11?

The search function in Windows 11 is a powerful tool for quickly finding files, applications, settings, and more. Here's how to use it effectively:

1. **Accessing Search:**

   o Click the **Search** icon (magnifying glass) on the taskbar.

   o Alternatively, press **Windows key + S** to open the Search pane.

   o You can also start typing directly on the desktop or in File Explorer to initiate a search.

2. **Searching for Files and Folders:**

   o Type the name of the file or folder you're looking for.

Chapter 1: User Interface & Navigation

- o As you type, Windows will display matching results categorized under **Apps**, **Documents**, **Web**, etc.

- o Click on the desired result to open it.

3. **Searching for Applications:**

- o Type the name of the application in the Search pane.

- o Applications are listed under the **Apps** category.

- o Click on the app to launch it.

4. **Using Advanced Search Operators:**

- o **File Type:** To search for a specific file type, use *.extension. For example, ***.pdf** searches for all PDF files.

- o **Date Modified:** Use date: followed by a date or relative term. Example: **date:this week**

- o **Size:** Use size: followed by size criteria. Example: **size:>100MB**

- o **Kind:** Specify the kind of item. Example: **kind:picture**

Examples:

- o **report *.docx date:this month** – Finds Word documents named "report" modified this month.

- o **budget size:>5MB** – Finds files named "budget" larger than 5MB.

5. **Searching Settings:**

- o To find specific settings, type keywords related to the setting.

- o For example, typing Bluetooth will display relevant settings under **System > Bluetooth & devices**.

6. **Web Search Integration:**

- o Windows 11 integrates web search results into the Search pane.

- o Scroll down to view **Web results**.

- o Clicking on a web result will open your default browser to the corresponding page.

7. **Voice Search:**

   o   If enabled, you can use voice commands by clicking the microphone icon in the Search pane.

   o   Speak your query, and Windows will process it accordingly.

8. **Refining Search Results:**

   o   Use filters available at the top of the Search pane to narrow down results by categories like **Documents**, **Apps**, **Web**, etc.

9. **Indexing Options (Optional):**

   o   To improve search performance, ensure that important folders are indexed.

   o   Open **Settings** > **Privacy & security** > **Searching Windows**.

   o   Under **Indexer status**, click **Advanced indexing options**.

   o   Adjust the indexed locations and rebuild the index if necessary.

Tips:

☐   **Be Specific:** Use specific keywords and operators to refine your searches.

☐   **Regular Indexing:** Keep your indexed locations updated for faster and more accurate search results.

How do I set up multiple monitors in Windows 11?

Setting up multiple monitors on Windows 11 can enhance your productivity and provide a more immersive computing experience.

Check Your Hardware

1.   Verify that your computer's graphics card has enough ports to support multiple monitors. If not, you may need additional adapters or a new graphics card.

Connect the Monitors to Your PC

1.   **Power Off Your PC:** It's safer to connect hardware while the computer is off.

2. **Connect Cables:**

☐ **HDMI:** Common for modern monitors; supports both video and audio.

☐ **DisplayPort:** Offers high performance for gaming and professional use.

☐ **DVI/VGA:** Older standards; may require adapters for newer systems.

3. **Power On Monitors:** Turn on each monitor and ensure they're set to the correct input source (e.g., HDMI 1, DisplayPort).

Power On and Detect Monitors

1. **Start Your PC:** Boot up your computer after all monitors are connected.

2. **Automatic Detection:** Windows 11 should automatically detect the connected monitors. If not:

☐ **Open Settings:** Press Win + I to open Settings.

☐ **Navigate to Display Settings:** Go to **System** > **Display**.

☐ **Detect:** Scroll down and click the **Detect** button under the **Multiple displays** section.

Configure Display Settings

Once all monitors are detected, you can customize their arrangement and settings:

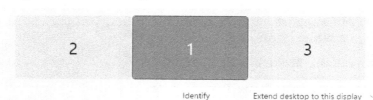

Identify   Extend desktop to this display ⌄

Arrange Your Displays

1. **Identify Displays:**

   ☐ In **Display Settings**, you'll see numbered boxes representing each monitor.

   ☐ Click **Identify** to see which number corresponds to which physical monitor.

2. **Drag and Drop:**

   ☐ Drag the monitor icons to match their physical arrangement on your desk (e.g., left, right, above).

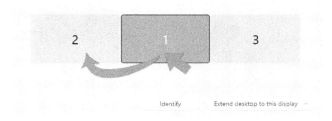

   ☐ This ensures smooth cursor movement between screens.

Choose Display Mode

Decide how you want to use the multiple monitors:

- **Extend These Displays:**

  ☐ **Purpose:** Expands your workspace across all screens.

  ☐ **How:** In **Display Settings**, under **Multiple displays**, select **Extend these displays** from the dropdown.

- **Duplicate These Displays:**

  ☐ **Purpose:** Shows the same content on all screens (useful for presentations).

  ☐ **How:** Select **Duplicate these displays**.

- **Show Only on 1 / Show Only on 2:**

  ☐ **Purpose:** Use only one monitor, turning off others.

27

☐ **How:** Choose **Show only on 1** or **Show only on 2** as needed.

Set the Primary Display

1. Select the monitor you want as the primary display.

2. Scroll down to **Multiple displays** and expand.

3. Check the box **Make this my main display**.

Adjust Resolution and Scaling

Scale & layout

⬚	Scale Change the size of text, apps, and other items	100% (Recommended) ˅ ›
⬚	Display resolution Adjust the resolution to fit your connected display	1920 × 1080 (Recommended) ˅
⬚	Display orientation	Landscape ˅

1. **Resolution:**

☐ Click on each monitor in **Display Settings**.

☐ Under **Scale & layout**, choose the desired **Display resolution** (recommended resolution is typically labeled as such).

2. **Scaling:**

☐ Adjust **Scale** to increase or decrease the size of text, apps, and other items.

☐ Common scaling options include 100%, 125%, 150%, etc.

Set Orientation

• Set each monitor's orientation (Landscape or Portrait) based on your preference or monitor setup.

How do I create custom keyboard shortcut?

Creating custom keyboard shortcuts can significantly enhance your productivity by allowing you to quickly access your favorite applications, files, or folders.

For Applications:

1. Open the Start Menu, locate the application you want to create a shortcut for.

2. Right click on the application icon, select "open file location."

3. Hold down shift, then right-click on the shortcut icon, then select "Properties."

4. In the Properties window, navigate to the "Shortcut" tab.

5. Click on the "Shortcut key" field. It will display "None" by default.

   Press the key combination you want to assign. Windows will automatically add Ctrl + Alt + before your chosen key. For example, pressing K will set the shortcut to Ctrl + Alt + K.

   Note: use combinations such as Ctrl + Alt + [Key], however avoid overriding existing system shortcuts as this can cause problems.

6. Click "Apply" and then "OK" to save your new keyboard shortcut.

How do I pin websites to the taskbar in Windows 11?

1. Open your preferred browser (e.g., Microsoft Edge, Chrome) and navigate to the desired website.

2. In Microsoft Edge:

   o Click the **three-dot menu** in the top-right corner.

   o Navigate to **More tools > Pin to taskbar**.

   o Confirm the action, and the website will appear as a taskbar icon.

3. For other browsers like Chrome:

   o Open the website, click the **three-dot menu**, and select **More tools > Create shortcut**.

   o Check the box for **Open as window** (optional) and click **Create**.

   o Right-click the shortcut and select **Pin to taskbar**.

Chapter 1: User Interface & Navigation

How do I navigate using keyboard shortcuts?

Keyboard shortcuts enhance productivity by allowing quick navigation and execution of tasks.

1. **Basic Shortcuts:**
   - o **Windows key:** Open or close the Start menu.
   - o **Windows key + D:** Show or hide the desktop.
   - o **Windows key + E:** Open File Explorer.
   - o **Windows key + I:** Open Settings.
   - o **Windows key + A:** Open Quick Settings.
   - o **Windows key + S:** Open Search.

2. **Window Management:**
   - o **Windows key + Arrow keys:** Snap windows to the sides or maximize/minimize.
   - o **Windows key + Tab:** Open Task View to switch between open apps and desktops.
   - o **Alt + Tab:** Switch between open applications.
   - o **Ctrl + Shift + Esc:** Open Task Manager.

3. **Accessibility Shortcuts:**
   - o **Windows key + Plus (+):** Open Magnifier and zoom in.
   - o **Windows key + Esc:** Exit Magnifier.
   - o **Windows key + U:** Open Accessibility settings.

4. **Virtual Desktops:**
   - o **Windows key + Ctrl + D:** Create a new virtual desktop.
   - o **Windows key + Ctrl + Left/Right Arrow:** Switch between virtual desktops.
   - o **Windows key + Ctrl + F4:** Close the current virtual desktop.

5. **Other Useful Shortcuts:**
   - o **Windows key + L:** Lock your PC.
   - o **Windows key + V:** Open Clipboard history (if enabled).
   - o **Windows key + G:** Open Xbox Game Bar for screen recording and gaming features.
   - o **Windows key + C:** Open Microsoft Teams chat (if enabled).

How Do I Adjust Volume in Windows 11?

Adjusting the volume in Windows 11 is straightforward and can be accomplished through various methods to suit your preferences and device setup. Whether you're using a desktop, laptop, or a device with built-in speakers or headphones, Windows 11 provides multiple avenues to control your audio levels effectively.

1. Using the Volume Icon on the Taskbar:

- **Locate the Volume Icon:**

  o Find the **Volume** icon (a speaker symbol) on the right side of the taskbar, near the system clock.

- **Adjust the Master Volume:**

  o **Click the Volume Icon:** Left-click the speaker icon to reveal quick settings.

  o **Move the Slider:** Drag the slider to the right to increase the volume or left to decrease it.

  o **Mute/Unmute:** Click the speaker icon at the top of the slider to mute or unmute the sound.

2. Utilizing Keyboard Shortcuts:

- **Identify Volume Keys:**

  o Many keyboards, especially on laptops, have dedicated volume keys often marked with speaker icons, typically found on the **Function (F1-F12)** keys.

- **Adjust Volume:**

  o **Increase Volume:** Press the **Volume Up** key (e.g., **Fn + F11**).

  o **Decrease Volume:** Press the **Volume Down** key (e.g., **Fn + F10**).

  o **Mute/Unmute:** Press the **Mute** key (e.g., **Fn + F9**).

Note: On some laptops, you may need to hold the **Fn** key while pressing the volume keys. Refer to your device's manual for specific key combinations.

3. Through the Settings App for Advanced Control:

- **Open Settings:**

Chapter 1: User Interface & Navigation

- o Press **Windows key + I** to open the **Settings** app.
- **Navigate to Sound Settings:**
  - o Click on **System** in the left-hand menu.
  - o Select **Sound** from the right pane.
- **Adjust Master Volume and Output Device:**
  - o Under **Output**, use the **Master volume** slider to set your preferred volume level.
  - o Choose your desired **Output** device (e.g., speakers, headphones) from the dropdown menu if multiple audio devices are connected.
- **Access Advanced Audio Options:**
  - o Scroll down to **Advanced** and click on **Volume mixer** to adjust individual application volumes separately. This is useful if you want certain apps to be louder or quieter than others.

4. **Using the Volume Mixer for Application-Specific Control:**

- **Open Volume Mixer:**
  - o Right-click the **Volume** icon on the taskbar and select **Open volume mixer**.

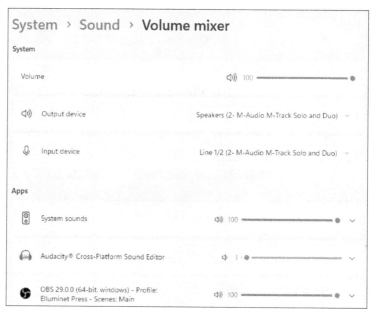

- **Adjust Individual Application Volumes:**

  o In the Volume Mixer window, you'll see sliders for each open application.

  o Drag the sliders right and left to increase or decrease the volume for each specific app independently.

How Do I Adjust Screen Brightness in Windows 11?

Adjusting the screen brightness in Windows 11 is essential for optimizing visibility, reducing eye strain, and conserving battery life on portable devices.

1. Using the Quick Settings Panel:

The Quick Settings panel provides a fast and convenient way to adjust screen brightness.

- **Access Quick Settings:**

  o Click on the **Quick Settings** icon located on the right side of the taskbar. It typically resembles a network, volume, or battery icon.

  o Alternatively, press **Windows key + A** to open the Quick Settings directly.

- **Adjust Brightness:**

  o In the Quick Settings panel, locate the **Brightness** slider.

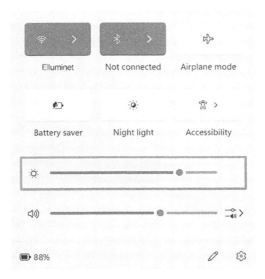

- o **Increase Brightness:** If you're on a laptop, drag the slider to the right to make the screen brighter.

- o **Decrease Brightness:** Drag the slider to the left to dim the screen.

- o **Toggle Adaptive Brightness (If Available):** Some devices offer an option to enable or disable adaptive brightness, which automatically adjusts the screen brightness based on ambient lighting. Click on the **Brightness** slider to toggle this feature on or off if available.

2

Settings & Personalization

How do I adjust display settings in Windows 11?

How do I switch between light and dark themes?

How do I customize the taskbar in Windows 11?

How do I change the screen resolution in Windows 11?

How do I change the desktop wallpaper in Windows 11?

How do I customize the lock screen in Windows 11?

How do I customize accent colors in Windows 11?

How do I adjust font accessibility settings?

How do I manage multiple desktops in Windows 11?

How do I configure notification settings in Windows 11?

How do I set up and manage virtual keyboards?

How do I customize the Start menu in Windows 11?

How do I manage themes in Windows 11?

How do I adjust power and sleep settings?

How do I configure privacy settings in Windows 11?

How do I customize the mouse cursor in Windows 11?

How do I customize the lock screen timeout settings?

How do I customize the lock screen in Windows 11?

How do I change system sounds in Windows 11?

How do I enable clipboard history in Windows 11?

How do I copy/cut and paste with the clipboard history?

How do I adjust display scaling for better readability?

How do I customize window animations & transitions?

Chapter 2: Settings & Personalization

How do I adjust display settings in Windows 11?

Adjusting display settings allows you to customize your screen resolution, scale, brightness, multiple displays, and more to enhance your visual experience.

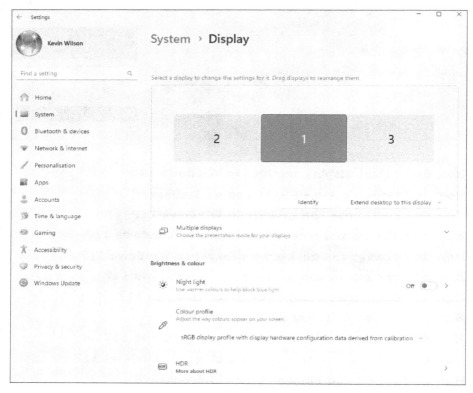

1. **Open Settings:** Press Win + I to open the Settings app.

2. **Navigate to Display Settings:** Click on *System* in the left sidebar and select *Display*.

3. **Change Display Resolution:** Under *Scale & layout*, click the dropdown next to *Display resolution* and select your desired resolution.

4. **Adjust Scaling:** In the *Scale & layout* section, choose a scaling percentage to increase or decrease the size of text, apps, and other items.

5. **Modify Orientation:** Under *Display orientation*, choose between *Landscape*, *Portrait*, *Landscape (flipped)*, or *Portrait (flipped)*.

6. **Manage Multiple Displays:** If you have multiple monitors, configure their arrangement by dragging and dropping the display icons under *Multiple displays*. Set the primary display by selecting the desired monitor and checking *Make this my main display*.

7. **Customize HDR and Advanced Settings (Optional):** If your display supports HDR, toggle it on under *Windows HD Color*. Explore *Advanced display settings* for more granular control over your display.

8. **Apply Changes:** After making adjustments, changes will apply automatically. Some changes may require you to sign out and back in or restart your PC.

9. **Use Night Light Feature:** Enable *Night light* under *Windows HD Color* to reduce blue light emission during evening hours, which can help reduce eye strain.

10. **Calibrate Display Colors (Optional):** Click on *Advanced display settings* and then *Color calibration* to adjust color settings for optimal display quality.

How do I switch between light and dark themes?

Switching between Light and Dark themes in Windows 11 allows you to customize the appearance of your operating system to suit your preferences and reduce eye strain, especially in different lighting conditions. Light theme uses bright interfaces with white or light-colored backgrounds. Dark theme features dark backgrounds with light-colored text and elements.

1. **Open Settings:** Press Win + I to open the Settings app.

2. **Navigate to Personalization:** Click on *Personalization* in the left sidebar.

3. **Select Colors:** Within Personalization, click on *Colors*.

4. **Choose Theme Mode:** Under *Choose your mode*, select *Light*, *Dark*, or *Custom*.

5. **Customize Further (If Needed):** If *Custom* is selected, you can independently set your *Choose your default Windows mode* and *Choose your default app mode* to either light or dark.

6. **Apply Changes:** The selected theme will apply immediately to system interfaces and supported applications.

Chapter 2: Settings & Personalization

7. **Set Different Themes for Apps:** Some applications have their own theme settings. Adjust these within the app settings if you prefer them to follow a different theme than the system.

8. **Use High Contrast Themes (Optional):** For enhanced visibility, select a high contrast theme under *Themes* in the Personalization settings.

9. **Change Accent Colors:** Customize accent colors to complement your chosen theme by selecting a color under *Accent color*.

10. **Revert to Default Themes (If Needed):** To return to the default theme settings, select *Windows default* under *Choose your mode*.

How do I customize the taskbar in Windows 11?

Customizing the taskbar allows you to personalize your desktop environment to better suit your workflow and aesthetic preferences.

1. Accessing Taskbar Settings

To begin customizing your taskbar:

1. **Right-Click Method:**

   o **Right-click** on an empty area of the **taskbar**.

   o Select **"Taskbar settings"** from the context menu.

2. **Settings App Method:**

   o Press **Win + I** to open the **Settings** app.

   o Navigate to **"Personalization"** in the sidebar.

   o Click on **"Taskbar"**.

2. Taskbar Alignment

Windows 11 allows you to align taskbar icons to the center or the left.

- In **Taskbar settings**, find the **"Taskbar behaviors"** section.

- Look for **"Taskbar alignment"**.

- Choose between **"Left"** or **"Center"** alignment based on your preference.

3. Personalizing Taskbar Appearance

1. Open Settings: Press **Win + I**.

2. Navigate to **"Personalization"** > **"Colors"**.

3. Choose your **accent color**:

   o **Automatic**: Windows selects a color based on your background.

   o **Manual Selection**: Pick a color from the palette or enter a hex code.

4. Toggle **"Transparency effects"** to **On** or **Off** to adjust the translucency of the taskbar and other UI elements.

4. Configuring Taskbar Behavior

In **Taskbar settings**, under **"Taskbar behaviors"**, you can adjust:

☐ **Automatically hide the taskbar**: Toggle this to hide the taskbar when not in use.

☐ **Select which icons appear on the taskbar**: Customize which system icons show in the notification area.

☐ **Show badges on taskbar apps**: Enable or disable badges (like unread counts) on taskbar icons.

☐ **Combine taskbar buttons**: Choose how multiple windows of the same app are displayed (always, when taskbar is full, never).

How do I change the screen resolution in Windows 11?

Changing the screen resolution in Windows 11 allows you to optimize your display for better clarity, performance, or to suit specific tasks like gaming, graphic design, or general productivity.

1. **Open Settings:** Press Win + I to open the Settings app.

2. **Navigate to Display Settings:** Click on *System* in the left sidebar and select *Display*.

3. **Change Display Resolution:** Under *Scale & layout*, locate *Display resolution*. Click the dropdown menu and select your desired resolution from the available options. Common resolutions include: 1920 x 1080 (Full HD), 2560 x 1440 (Quad HD), 3840 x 2160 (4K UHD)

4. **Confirm Changes:** After selecting a new resolution, a prompt will appear asking if you want to keep the changes. Click *Keep changes* if the display looks correct. If not, it will revert after 15 seconds.

5. **Adjust Scaling:** In the same *Scale & layout* section, adjust the scaling percentage if necessary to ensure text and apps are appropriately sized.

6. **Set Primary Display (If Using Multiple Monitors):** Click on the monitor you want to set as primary. Scroll down and check *Make this my main display*.

7. **Apply Changes:** The settings will apply automatically. Some changes may require you to sign out and back in or restart your PC.

8. **Use Advanced Display Settings (Optional):** Click on *Advanced display* for more detailed configuration options, such as refresh rate and color calibration.

9. **Calibrate Display Colors (Optional):** In *Advanced display settings*, select *Color calibration* to adjust color settings for optimal display quality.

10. **Troubleshoot Resolution Issues (If Needed):** If you encounter problems with display resolution, ensure your graphics drivers are up to date via *Device Manager* under *Display adapters*.

How do I change the desktop wallpaper in Windows 11?

Changing the desktop wallpaper allows you to personalize your computer's appearance to match your style and preferences. You can to use a built-in image, a personal photo, or even a dynamic slideshow,

1. **Open Settings:**
   o Press **Win + I** to launch the **Settings** app.

2. **Navigate to Personalization:**
   o In the left sidebar, click on **Personalization**.

3. **Select Background:**
   o Within Personalization, click on **Background**.

4. **Choose Background Type:**
   o Under **Personalize your background**, select from the dropdown menu:

- **Picture**: Use a single image as your wallpaper.

- **Solid color**: Choose a solid color.

- **Slideshow**: Rotate through a folder of images.

5. **Set a Picture as Wallpaper:**

   o If you selected **Picture**:

      - Click **Browse** to choose an image from your computer.

      - Select the desired image and click **Choose picture**.

6. **Set a Solid Color:**

   o If you selected **Solid color**:

      - Choose your preferred color from the palette.

7. **Set a Slideshow:**

   o If you selected **Slideshow**:

      - Click **Browse** to select a folder containing your preferred images.

      - Adjust settings like **Change picture every** and **Shuffle the picture order** as desired.

8. **Adjust Fit:**

   o Under **Choose a fit**, select how the image fits on your screen (e.g., Fill, Fit, Stretch, Tile, Center, Span).

9. **Preview and Apply:**

   o Your changes will preview automatically. Once satisfied, simply close the Settings app.

How do I customize the lock screen in Windows 11?

Customizing the lock screen in Windows 11 allows you to personalize the initial screen that appears when you wake your device or sign in. By tailoring the lock screen settings, you can display your favorite photos, show important notifications, and choose how information such as calendar events or weather updates appear.

1. **Open Settings:**

   o Press **Win + I** to open the **Settings** app.

Chapter 2: Settings & Personalization

2. **Navigate to Personalization:**

   o Click on **Personalization** in the left sidebar.

3. **Select Lock Screen:**

   o Within Personalization, click on **Lock screen**.

4. **Choose Background Type:**

   o Under **Personalize your lock screen**, select from:

      ▪ **Windows spotlight**: Dynamic images curated by Microsoft.

      ▪ **Picture**: Use a specific image.

      ▪ **Slideshow**: Rotate through a folder of images.

5. **Set a Specific Picture:**

   o If you choose **Picture**:

      ▪ Click **Browse** to select an image from your computer.

      ▪ Choose your desired image and click **Choose picture**.

6. **Set a Slideshow:**

   o If you choose **Slideshow**:

      ▪ Click **Add a folder** to select a folder containing your preferred images.

      ▪ Adjust settings like **Change picture every** as needed.

7. **Customize Lock Screen Apps:**

   o Scroll down to **Show lock screen status for apps**.

   o Toggle on the apps you want to display status information (e.g., Calendar, Mail).

8. **Advanced Background Settings (Optional):**

   o Toggle **Show lock screen background picture on the sign-in screen** to **On** or **Off** based on your preference.

9. **Apply Changes:**

o   Changes apply automatically. Close the Settings app when done.

How do I customize accent colors in Windows 11?

Accent colors are applied to various user interface (UI) elements such as the Start menu, taskbar, window borders, and buttons.

1. **Open Settings:**

   o   Press **Win + I** to launch the **Settings** app.

2. **Navigate to Personalization:**

   o   Click on **Personalization** in the left sidebar.

3. **Select Colors:**

   o   Within Personalization, click on **Colors**.

4. **Choose Accent Color:**

   o   Scroll down to the **Accent color** section.

   o   Select a color from the predefined palette or click **View colors** for more options.

5. **Automatic Accent Color from Background (Optional):**

   o   Toggle on **Automatically pick an accent color from my background** to let Windows choose a color based on your desktop background.

6. **Show Accent Color on Surfaces:**

   o   Choose where the accent color applies:

      ▪   **Start and taskbar**

      ▪   **Title bars and window borders**

      ▪   **Buttons and other elements**

7. **Custom Accent Colors:**

   o   To select a custom color, click **Custom color** and use the color picker to choose your desired shade.

8. **Transparency Effects (Optional):**

   o   Toggle on **Transparency effects** to apply a translucent look to accent-colored surfaces.

9. **Apply Changes:**

   o   Your selected accent color will apply immediately across supported system interfaces and applications.

How do I adjust font accessibility settings?

Adjusting font settings in Windows 11 can enhance readability and personalize your user experience.

1. **Open Settings:**

   o   Press **Win + I** to open the **Settings** app.

2. **Navigate to Accessibility:**

   o   Click on **Accessibility** in the left sidebar.

3. **Select Text Size:**

   o   Under **Vision**, click on **Text size**.

4. **Adjust Text Size:**

   o   Use the slider to increase or decrease the text size system-wide.

   o   A preview will show the change in real-time.

5. **Apply Changes:**

   o   Click **Apply** to implement the new text size settings.

6. **Advanced Font Settings (Optional):**

   o   For more granular font customization, click on **Advanced scaling settings** under the **Display** section.

   o   Note: Windows 11 has limited native options for font customization. For extensive changes, consider third-party tools or registry edits, but proceed with caution.

7. **Use ClearType Text Tuner (Optional):**

   o   Type **ClearType** in the Start menu search and select **Adjust ClearType text**.

   o   Follow the on-screen instructions to fine-tune text clarity.

How do I manage multiple desktops in Windows 11?

Managing multiple desktops in Windows 11 is a powerful way to organize your workspace, enhance productivity, and keep different tasks separated. These are called virtual desktops.

Virtual Desktops are separate instances of the desktop environment that allow you to organize open applications and windows into distinct spaces. Each virtual desktop can host its own set of applications, helping you reduce clutter and focus on specific tasks without interference from other activities.

1. **Open Task View:**

   o Press **Win + Tab** or click the **Task View** button on the taskbar (usually next to the Start button).

2. **Add a New Desktop:**

   o In the Task View interface, click on **New desktop** at the bottom of the screen.

3. **Switch Between Desktops:**

   o Press **Ctrl + Win + Left/Right Arrow** to switch between multiple desktops.

   o Alternatively, use the Task View to select the desired desktop.

4. **Rename a Desktop (Optional):**

   o In Task View, right-click on the desktop you want to rename.

   o Select **Rename** and enter the new name.

5. **Move Windows Between Desktops:**

   o Open Task View by pressing **Win + Tab**.

   o Drag and drop the desired window from one desktop to another.

6. **Close a Desktop:**

   o In Task View, hover over the desktop you wish to close and click the **X** button.

   o Any open windows on that desktop will move to the previous desktop.

Chapter 2: Settings & Personalization

7. Customize Each Desktop (Optional):

- Each desktop can have its own set of open applications and background settings.

- Switch to the desired desktop and customize it as needed.

How do I configure notification settings in Windows 11?

Configuring notification settings in Windows 11 allows you to manage how and when you receive alerts from the system and various applications. Properly managing notifications can help reduce distractions, improve productivity, and ensure you stay informed about important updates.

1. Open Settings:

- Press **Win + I** to launch the **Settings** app.

2. Navigate to Notifications:

- Click on **System** in the left sidebar.

- Select **Notifications**.

3. Manage Global Notifications:

- Toggle **Notifications** to **On** or **Off** to enable or disable all notifications.

4. Customize Individual App Notifications:

- Scroll down to **Notifications from apps and other senders**.

- Toggle notifications **On** or **Off** for each listed app.

5. Configure Notification Behavior:

- **Show notifications on the lock screen**: Toggle to show or hide notifications on the lock screen.

- **Notification banners**: Choose whether notifications appear as banners on the screen.

- **Show notifications in action center**: Toggle to display notifications in the Action Center.

6. Set Focus Assist Rules:

o   Click on **Focus assist** within the Notifications settings.

o   Choose between **Off**, **Priority only**, or **Alarms only**.

o   Customize automatic rules for when Focus Assist activates (e.g., during specific times, when duplicating displays, or while playing games).

7. Adjust Notification Sounds:

o   Scroll down to **Notification sounds**.

o   Toggle **Play a sound when a notification arrives** to **On** or **Off**.

8. Notification Previews:

o   Under **Notification messages**, choose between **Always show**, **Hide sensitive information**, or **Never show** previews.

9. Apply Changes:

o   All adjustments apply immediately. Close the Settings app when done.

How do I set up and manage virtual keyboards?

Setting up and managing virtual keyboards in Windows 11 can enhance your typing experience, provide accessibility options, and offer flexibility for various devices like tablets and touch-enabled PCs.

1. Open Settings:

o   Press **Win + I** to open the **Settings** app.

2. Navigate to Accessibility:

o   Click on **Accessibility** in the left sidebar.

3. Select Keyboard:

o   Under **Interaction**, click on **Keyboard**.

4. Enable On-Screen Keyboard:

o   Toggle **On-Screen Keyboard** to **On**.

o   The virtual keyboard will appear on your screen, allowing you to type using your mouse or touch.

5. **Customize Keyboard Settings:**

   o **Use the On-Screen Keyboard**: Toggle to show or hide the keyboard.

   o **Keyboard shortcuts**: Review and customize shortcuts related to keyboard usage.

6. **Add Additional Input Methods (Optional):**

   o Go back to **Settings** and select **Time & language**.

   o Click on **Language & region**.

   o Under **Preferred languages**, select your language and click **Options**.

   o Click **Add a keyboard** to include additional keyboard layouts or input methods.

7. **Switch Between Keyboards:**

   o Press **Win + Spacebar** to cycle through installed keyboard layouts.

8. **Remove Unwanted Keyboards:**

   o In **Language & region**, under **Preferred languages**, select the language and click **Options**.

   o Under **Keyboards**, click on the keyboard you want to remove and select **Remove**.

9. **Apply Changes:**

   o Changes take effect immediately. Close the Settings app when finished.

How do I customize the Start menu in Windows 11?

Windows 11 introduces a redesigned Start menu that emphasizes simplicity and ease of access. Unlike its predecessor, the Start menu in Windows 11 is centered by default and features a streamlined interface that focuses on pinned applications, recent documents and apps.

1. **Open Settings:**

   o Press **Win + I** to launch the **Settings** app.

2. **Navigate to Personalization:**

o Click on **Personalization** in the left sidebar.

3. Select Start:

o Within Personalization, click on **Start**.

4. Customize Start Menu Items:

o Toggle on or off the following options to show or hide items on the Start menu:

- **Pinned apps**

- **Recent apps**

- **Most used apps**

- **Recently added apps**

- **Show recently opened items in Start, Jump Lists, and File Explorer**

5. Manage Pinned Apps:

o **Pin an App:**

- Open the **Start menu** by clicking the **Start** button or pressing **Win**.

- Right-click on the desired app and select **Pin to Start**.

o **Unpin an App:**

- Open the **Start menu**.

- Right-click on the app you want to remove and select **Unpin from Start**.

6. Adjust Start Menu Layout:

o Currently, Windows 11 offers limited customization for the Start menu layout. For advanced customization, consider third-party tools like **StartAllBack** or **Start11**.

7. Set Start Menu Alignment:

o Go back to **Personalization** > **Taskbar** > **Taskbar behaviors**.

o Under **Taskbar alignment**, choose between **Center** or **Left** to align the Start button accordingly.

8. **Apply Changes:**

    o   Your Start menu customizations apply immediately. Close the Settings app when done.

How do I manage themes in Windows 11?

Themes in Windows 11 are preset templates that change the appearance of the operating system to create a cohesive and personalized look. By altering various visual elements such as wallpapers, colors, sounds, and cursor styles, themes allow users to tailor their computing environment to their aesthetic preferences and functional needs.

1. **Open Settings:**

    o   Press **Win + I** to open the **Settings** app.

2. **Navigate to Personalization:**

    o   Click on **Personalization** in the left sidebar.

3. **Select Themes:**

    o   Within Personalization, click on **Themes**.

4. **Choose a Preinstalled Theme:**

    o   Under **Apply a theme**, select from the available themes such as **Windows**, **Dark**, **Light**, or other preinstalled options.

5. **Download More Themes:**

    o   Click on **Browse themes** to visit the Microsoft Store and download additional themes.

6. **Customize Current Theme:**

    o   **Background**: Change wallpaper by selecting **Background** under Themes.

    o   **Color**: Adjust accent colors under **Colors**.

    o   **Sounds**: Modify system sounds by selecting **Sounds**.

    o   **Mouse Cursor**: Change the cursor style by selecting **Mouse cursor**.

7. **Create a Custom Theme:**

    o   After customizing background, colors, sounds, and

cursor:

- Return to **Themes**.
- Click **Save theme**.
- Enter a name for your custom theme and click **Save**.

8. **Apply a Custom Theme:**

   o In **Themes**, under **Apply a theme**, select your saved custom theme from the list.

9. **Revert to Default Themes (If Needed):**

   o To return to the default Windows themes, select **Windows** or another default option under **Apply a theme**.

10. **Apply Changes:**

    o Your selected theme will apply immediately. Close the Settings app when finished.

How do I adjust power and sleep settings?

Adjusting power and sleep settings in Windows 11 is essential for optimizing your device's energy consumption, enhancing performance, and prolonging battery life. These settings allow you to control how your computer behaves when it's idle, determine when the screen turns off, and configure sleep modes to suit your usage patterns.

1. **Open Settings:**

   o Press **Win + I** to launch the **Settings** app.

2. **Navigate to System:**

   o Click on **System** in the left sidebar.

3. **Select Power & Battery:**

   o Within System, click on **Power & battery**.

4. **Adjust Screen and Sleep Settings:**

   o Under **Power**, expand **Screen and sleep**.

   o Configure the following options:

- **On battery power, turn off my screen after**: Choose the duration before the screen turns off when on battery.

- **When plugged in, turn off my screen after**: Set the duration for when the device is plugged in.

- **On battery power, put my device to sleep after**: Define when the device should sleep on battery.

- **When plugged in, put my device to sleep after**: Set sleep duration when plugged in.

5. **Configure Power Mode:**

   o   Under **Power mode**, select from options like **Best power efficiency**, **Balanced**, or **Best performance** to optimize power usage based on your needs.

6. **Battery Saver Settings (Optional):**

   o   Toggle **Battery saver** on or off.

   o   Click **Battery saver settings** to customize when Battery saver activates and which apps are restricted.

7. **Additional Power Settings:**

   o   Scroll down and click **Additional power settings** to open the **Power Options** in the Control Panel.

   o   Here, you can choose or customize a power plan, adjust advanced power settings, and configure sleep timers.

8. **Apply Changes:**

   o   All adjustments take effect immediately. Close the Settings app when done.

How do I configure privacy settings in Windows 11?

Configuring privacy settings is crucial for safeguarding your personal information and ensuring that your data is handled according to your preferences. Windows 11 features a comprehensive suite of privacy controls that allow you to manage how the operating system and installed applications access and use your data.

Chapter 2: Settings & Personalization

1. **Open Settings:**

   o   Press **Win + I** to launch the **Settings** app.

2. **Navigate to Privacy & security:**

   o   Click on **Privacy & security** in the left sidebar.

3. **General Privacy Settings:**

   o   Under **General**, manage options such as:

   ▪   **Let apps show notifications on the lock screen**

   ▪   **Send Microsoft information about how I write**

   ▪   **Let Windows track app launches to improve Start and search results**

4. **App Permissions:**

   o   Scroll down to **App permissions** and configure permissions for:

   ▪   **Location**
   ▪   **Camera**
   ▪   **Microphone**
   ▪   **Notifications**
   ▪   **Account info**
   ▪   **Contacts**
   ▪   **Calendar**
   ▪   **Call history**
   ▪   **Email**
   ▪   **Tasks**
   ▪   **Messaging**
   ▪   **Radio**
   ▪   **Motion**
   ▪   **File system**
   ▪   **Documents**
   ▪   **Pictures**
   ▪   **Videos**
   ▪   **Bluetooth**
   ▪   **Accounts**
   ▪   **Background apps**
   ▪   **App diagnostics**

5. **Adjust Specific Permissions:**

   o   Click on each permission category (e.g., **Camera**) to

toggle access **On** or **Off** for individual apps.

6. **Windows Permissions:**

   o   Configure settings for **Diagnostics & feedback**, **Activity history**, and **Windows permissions** such as **Location**, **Camera**, and **Microphone**.

7. **Privacy Dashboard (Optional):**

   o   Click **Privacy Dashboard** to view and manage data collected by Microsoft, including activity history, location activity, and diagnostic data.

8. **Tailor Permissions for Specific Apps:**

   o   For enhanced privacy, review each app's permissions and disable access where unnecessary.

9. **Apply Changes:**

   o   Adjustments take effect immediately. Close the Settings app when finished.

How do I customize the mouse cursor in Windows 11?

Customizing the mouse cursor allows you to personalize your computing experience, enhance visibility, and improve accessibility based on your individual preferences and needs. Whether you want to change the cursor's size, color, shape, or add animation effects, Windows 11 provides a variety of built-in options and supports third-party themes to help you achieve the perfect look.

1. **Open Settings:**

   o   Press **Win + I** to launch the **Settings** app.

2. **Navigate to Accessibility:**

   o   Click on **Accessibility** in the left sidebar.

3. **Select Mouse Pointer and Touch:**

   o   Under **Interaction**, click on **Mouse pointer and touch**.

4. **Change Pointer Size and Color:**

   o   **Pointer size**: Use the slider to increase or decrease the cursor size.

   o   **Pointer color**: Choose from predefined colors or select

Custom to pick your own.

5. **Enable or Disable Pointer Trails (Optional):**

   o   Click on **Additional mouse settings** at the bottom.

   o   In the **Mouse Properties** window, go to the **Pointer Options** tab.

   o   Check or uncheck **Display pointer trails** as desired.

   o   Click **Apply** and **OK** to confirm changes.

6. **Use Custom Cursor Schemes (Optional):**

   o   Download custom cursor schemes from trusted sources.

   o   In **Mouse Properties** > **Pointers**, click **Browse** to locate and apply custom cursor files.

7. **Apply Changes:**

   o   Customizations take effect immediately. Close the Settings or Mouse Properties window when done.

How do I customize the lock screen timeout settings?

Customizing the lock screen timeout settings in Windows 11 allows you to control how long your device remains active before automatically locking or entering sleep mode. By adjusting these settings, you can enhance both the security and energy efficiency of your computer, ensuring that it locks promptly when not in use or remains active for longer periods based on your preferences.

1. **Open Settings:**

   o   Press **Win + I** to launch the **Settings** app.

2. **Navigate to System:**

   o   Click on **System** in the left sidebar.

3. **Select Power & Battery:**

   o   Within System, click on **Power & battery**.

4. **Adjust Screen and Sleep Settings:**

   o   Under **Power**, expand the **Screen and sleep** section.

   o   Configure the following options:

- **On battery power, turn off my screen after**: Set the duration of inactivity before the screen turns off when running on battery.

- **When plugged in, turn off my screen after**: Define the timeout duration when connected to a power source.

- **On battery power, put my device to sleep after**: Choose when the device should enter sleep mode on battery.

- **When plugged in, put my device to sleep after**: Set sleep mode timeout when plugged in.

5. **Advanced Power Settings (Optional)**:

   o Click **Additional power settings** to open the **Power Options** in the Control Panel.

   o Select **Change plan settings** next to your active power plan.

   o Click **Change advanced power settings** to access more detailed timeout and power management options.

6. **Apply Changes**:

   o Adjustments take effect immediately. Close the Settings app when finished.

How do I customize the lock screen in Windows 11?

1. Press **Win + I** to open the Settings app and navigate to **Personalization > Lock screen**.

2. Click the dropdown menu under **Personalize your lock screen** to select:

   o **Windows Spotlight** for rotating images curated by Microsoft.

   o **Picture** to use a custom image as your lock screen background.

   o **Slideshow** to display a slideshow of selected photos.

3. If you choose **Picture**, click **Browse photos**, navigate to your desired image, and click **Choose picture**.

4. If you select **Slideshow**, click **Add a folder**, choose a folder containing your desired images, and click **Choose this folder**.

5. Enable or disable **Get fun facts, tips, tricks, and more on your lock screen** depending on your preference for additional information.

6. Configure lock screen apps by clicking on the app icon under **Choose an app to show detailed status**. Select an app such as Calendar or Weather to display its updates on the lock screen.

How do I change system sounds in Windows 11?

Changing system sounds in Windows 11 allows you to personalize your computing experience by customizing the audio feedback for various system events such as notifications, errors, and actions.

1. Press **Win + I** to open the Settings app and navigate to **System > Sound**.

2. Scroll down to **Advanced sound options** and click **More sound settings**.

3. In the Sound settings window, switch to the **Sounds tab**.

4. Under **Program Events**, select the event (e.g., Notification, Device Connect) for which you want to change the sound.

5. Click the **Browse** button under the **Sounds** drop down box, navigate to a custom audio file (in WAV format), and select it.

6. Click **Test** to preview the sound, then click **Apply** and **OK** to save your changes.

How do I enable clipboard history in Windows 11?

Clipboard History is a feature in Windows 11 that stores multiple items you've copied to the clipboard, allowing you to access and paste them later. This includes text snippets, images, and other types of content. By default, the clipboard only holds the most recent item you've copied

1. Press **Win + I** to open the Settings app and navigate to **System > Clipboard**.

2. Toggle on **Clipboard history** to allow Windows to save multiple copied items.

3. Press **Win + V** to open the clipboard history interface.

4. Click on any item in the clipboard history to paste it into the current application.

5. Use the **Pin** icon next to frequently used items to keep them saved even after restarting your PC.

How do I copy/cut and paste with the clipboard history?

Clipboard history allows you to access a list of previously copied or cut items, enabling you to paste them at your convenience without the need to recopy them.

Copying Items:

- Select the text, image, or file you want to copy.

- Press **Ctrl + C** to copy the selected item to the clipboard.

Cutting Items:

- Select the text, image, or file you want to cut.

- Press **Ctrl + X** to cut the selected item, removing it from its original location and placing it in the clipboard.

Pasting Items:

Once you've copied or cut multiple items, you can access your clipboard history to view and select from previously stored content.

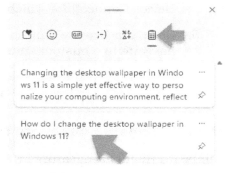

- **Press Win + V** to open the clipboard history

- Browse through the list of copied or cut items.

- The selected item will be pasted into your current cursor location in the active application.

How do I adjust display scaling for better readability?

Adjusting display scaling in Windows 11 is an effective way to enhance readability and ensure that text, apps, and other visual elements are comfortably sized according to your preferences and display resolution. Whether you're using a high-resolution monitor, a laptop with a small screen, or require larger text for better visibility

Chapter 2: Settings & Personalization

1. Press **Win + I** to open the Settings app and navigate to **System > Display**.

2. Scroll down to the **Scale and layout** section.

3. Use the dropdown menu under **Scale** to select a preset percentage:

   o   100% for default scaling.

   o   125% or 150% for larger text and UI elements.

4. If no preset works, click **Advanced scaling settings** and enter a custom scaling value between 100% and 500%.

5. Restart your computer after applying a custom scaling value for it to take effect.

6. If blurry text appears, toggle **Fix scaling for apps** in the **Advanced scaling settings** menu.

How do I customize window animations & transitions?

Customizing window animations and transitions in Windows 11 allows you to tailor the visual experience of your operating system to better suit your preferences and performance needs.

Disabling animations in Windows can lead to a more streamlined and responsive user experience, especially on older hardware or devices with limited resources. Animations, while visually appealing, can sometimes cause distractions or slow down system performance.

1. **Open Settings:**

   o   Click the **Start** button and select **Settings**.

   o   Alternatively, press **Windows key + I** to open Settings directly.

2. **Navigate to Accessibility Settings:**

   o   In the Settings window, click on **Accessibility** from the left-hand menu.

3. **Access Visual Effects:**

   o   Within Accessibility, select **Visual effects**.

4. **Adjust Animation Settings:**

   o   **Transparency effects:**

- Toggle **Transparency effects** on or off to enable or disable semi-transparent elements like the Start menu, taskbar, and Action Center.

    o **Animation effects:**

    - Toggle **Animation effects** on or off to enable or disable window animations and transitions.

5. **Advanced Animation Settings (Optional):**

    o For more granular control over animations, you may need to adjust settings via the Registry Editor or use third-party tools. **Note:** Modifying the registry can be risky; proceed with caution or seek professional assistance.

6. **Apply Changes:**

    o Once you've adjusted the settings, close the Settings window. Changes should take effect immediately.

Tips:

- Disabling animations can improve system performance, especially on older hardware.

- Enabling transparency effects can make the interface look more modern but may slightly impact performance.

How do I install fonts?

Installing new fonts allows you to personalize and enhance the visual appeal of your text in various applications, such as word processors, graphic design software, or presentation tools.

There are many reliable sources to download fonts. Always download fonts from trusted sources to avoid malware or copyright issues.

1. **Microsoft Store**:

    o Offers paid and free fonts that cover basic design and language needs.

2. **Online Font Libraries**:

    o **Google Fonts** (fonts.google.com):

    - Offers a vast collection of free fonts for personal and commercial use.

- o **DaFont** (dafont.com):
  - ▪ Provides decorative, thematic, and niche fonts for personal projects.

- o **Font Squirrel** (fontsquirrel.com):
  - ▪ Features high-quality fonts that are free for commercial use.

Method 1: Using the Settings App

1. **Open Settings**:
   - o Press Win + I to open the Settings app.

2. **Navigate to Personalization**:
   - o Go to **Personalization** > **Fonts**.

3. **Install Fonts**:
   - o Drag and drop the font file(s) into the box that says, "Drag and drop to install." Alternatively, click **Browse fonts** to locate and select your font file(s) for installation.
   - o You can also click "get more fonts in Microsoft Store" and browse through the available fonts.

Method 2: Using File Explorer

1. **Download the Font(s)**:
   - o Ensure you have downloaded the font files (.ttf, .otf, or .fon formats) from a trusted source.
   - o Sometimes, fonts are downloaded as a .zip archive to bundle multiple font files together. If this is the case, you'll need to extract the font files before installing them (right click on .zip file, select "extract all".

2. **Locate the Font Files**:
   - o Navigate to the folder where the downloaded font files are stored.

3. **Select the Fonts**:
   - o If you want to install multiple fonts, hold down the Ctrl key and click on each font file to select them, or use Ctrl + A to select all the fonts in the folder.

Chapter 2: Settings & Personalization

4. Install the Fonts:

- ○ **Right-Click and Install**:

  - ▪ Right-click on the selected font files and choose **Install** (for just your account) or **Install for all users**. Select "Install for all users", this will install the fonts in C:\Windows\Fonts.

How do I change the system date and time?

Changing the time and date on your Windows 11 device might be necessary for various reasons. For example, if you are traveling to a different time zone and your device does not automatically update to the local time, manually adjusting it ensures accurate scheduling and synchronization.

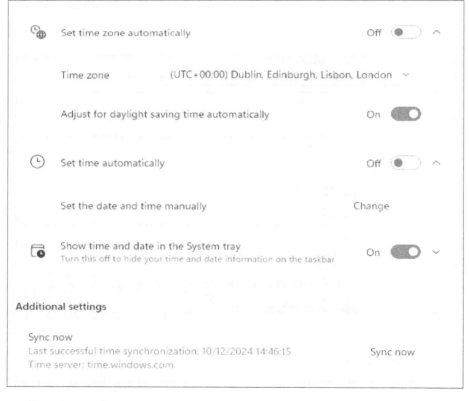

1. Open the Date & Time Settings:

- ○ Go to **Settings** by pressing Windows + I.

o   Navigate to **Time & language > Date & time**.

2. **Disable Automatic Time Settings**:

    o   In the settings panel, turn off the toggle for **Set the time zone automatically** if it is currently enabled. This will allow you to make manual adjustments.

3. **Set the Time Zone**:

    o   Select your correct **Time zone** from the dropdown menu if it doesn't match your location.

4. **Adjust for Daylight Saving Time**:

    o   Ensure the **Adjust for daylight saving time automatically** option is enabled if your region follows daylight saving changes.

5. **Show Time in the System Tray**:

    o   The option **Show time and date in the System tray** ensures the time is visible on the taskbar. You can toggle this setting based on your preference.

6. **Synchronize the Clock**:

    o   To ensure the system time is accurate, use the **Sync now** button under **Additional settings**. This will synchronize your time with an online server.

7. **Manually Set the Date and Time (if necessary)**:

    o   If automatic time synchronization is disabled, you can manually change the date and time:

        ▪   Turn off **Set time automatically** if it's enabled.

        ▪   Click **Change** under **Set the date and time manually**, then enter the correct date and time.

8. **Show Additional Calendars (Optional)**:

    o   You can enable additional calendar displays in the taskbar using the **Show additional calendars in the taskbar** dropdown menu.

How do I change keyboard layout and language?

Changing the keyboard layout and language allows you to type in different languages or use alternative keyboard layouts.

Chapter 2: Settings & Personalization

Add a Keyboard Layout or Language

1. **Open Settings**:

   o Press Windows + I or click the **Start** button and select **Settings**.

2. **Go to Language Settings**:

   o In the left-hand menu, select **Time & language**.

   o Click **Language & region** on the right.

3. **Add a Language**:

   o Under the **Preferred languages** section, click **Add a language**.

   o Search for the language you want to add, select it, and click **Next**.

   o Choose additional features such as speech recognition or handwriting, if needed, and click **Install**.

4. **Add a Keyboard Layout**:

   o After the language is installed, click the three dots (...) next to the language in the **Preferred languages** list and select **Language options**.

   o Scroll down to **Keyboards** and click **Add a keyboard**.

   o Select the desired keyboard layout from the list.

Switch Between Keyboard Layouts or Languages

1. **Using the Language Switcher**:

   o Press Windows + Spacebar to quickly toggle between installed keyboard layouts or languages.

   o Alternatively, click the **Language icon** in the taskbar (near the clock) and select the desired language.

2. **Using a Keyboard Shortcut**:

   o Press Shift + Alt (default) or Ctrl + Shift to cycle through installed layouts.

   o You can configure these shortcuts in **Settings > Time & language > Typing > Advanced keyboard settings**.

Set a Default Keyboard Layout

1. **Open Advanced Keyboard Settings**:

   o   Go to **Settings > Time & language > Typing**.

   o   Click **Advanced keyboard settings** under **More keyboard settings**.

2. **Select the Default Layout**:

   o   Use the **Override for default input method** dropdown menu to choose the default language and keyboard layout.

Remove a Keyboard Layout or Language

1. **Go to Language Options**:

   o   Open **Settings > Time & language > Language & region**.

   o   Click the three dots (...) next to the language and select **Language options**.

2. **Remove the Keyboard Layout**:

   o   Under **Keyboards**, click on the layout you want to remove and select **Remove**.

3. **Remove the Language**:

   o   Back in the **Preferred languages** section, click the three dots (...) next to the language and select **Remove**.

How do I change language and region?

Changing the language and region in Windows 11 can help you customize your system to match your preferences, such as displaying the interface in a different language, using specific regional formats, or accessing region-specific features.

Change the Display Language

1. **Open Settings**:

   o   Press Windows + I or click the **Start** button and select **Settings**.

2. **Go to Language Settings**:

    o   In the left-hand menu, click **Time & language**.

    o   Select **Language & region**.

3. **Add a New Language**:

    o   Under the **Preferred languages** section, click **Add a language**.

    o   Search for the language you want to add using the search bar.

    o   Select the language from the list and click **Next**.

    o   Choose any additional features you'd like to install (e.g., Speech, Handwriting) and click **Install**.

4. **Set as Display Language**:

    o   Once the language is installed, click the three dots (...) next to the language in the **Preferred languages** list and select **Move up** to make it the default.

    o   If prompted, log out and log back in to apply the changes.

Change the Region

1. **Open Region Settings**:

    o   In the same **Language & region** settings page, scroll down to the **Region** section.

2. **Select Your Region**:

    o   Under **Country or region**, select your desired country or region from the dropdown list.

3. **Adjust Regional Format**:

    o   If your region uses a different date, time, or currency format than you prefer, you can manually adjust it:

        ▪   Click the **Regional format** dropdown and select a format.

        ▪   If needed, click **Change formats** to customize individual settings such as the short date, long date, time format, or first day of the week.

Remove a Language or Change Priority

1. **Go to Language & Region Settings**:

   o Navigate to **Settings > Time & language > Language & region**.

2. **Remove a Language**:

   o Click the three dots (...) next to a language in the **Preferred languages** section and select **Remove**.

3. **Reorder Languages**:

   o Use the **Move up** and **Move down** options next to the language to set the order of preference for language packs.

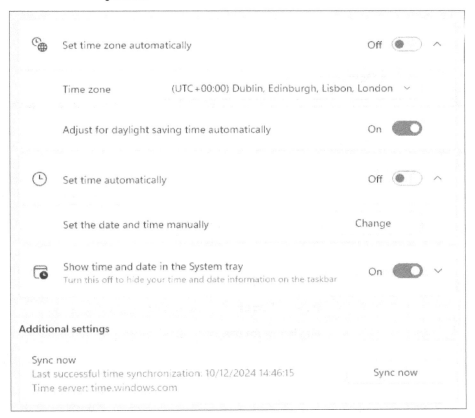

Chapter 2: Settings & Personalization

How do I create a custom Power Plan?

Custom power plans allow you to optimize your system's power usage based on your preferences, such as prioritizing performance or battery life.

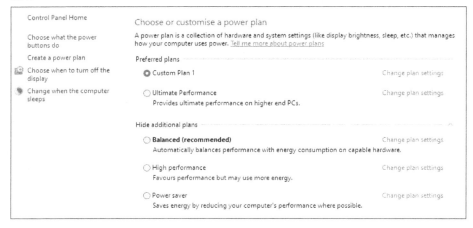

1. **Open Power Options**:

   o   Press Windows + R on your keyboard to open the **Run** dialog box.

   o   Type **powercfg.cpl**

2. **Create a New Power Plan**:

   o   In the left-hand menu, click **Create a power plan**.

   o   Select a base plan (e.g., Balanced, Power Saver, or High Performance) as a starting point.

      ▯   **Balanced**: Optimizes performance with energy consumption.

      ▯   **Power Saver**: Prioritizes energy efficiency.

      ▯   **High Performance**: Maximizes performance but uses more energy.

   o   Enter a name for your custom plan and click **Next**.

3. **Choose sleep and display settings**

   o   Set amount of time before display turns off

   o   Set amount of time before computer goes to sleep

   o   Click **create**.

4. Configure Power Settings:

   ○ Click **Change Plan Settings** next to your plan.

   ○ Click **Change advanced power settings**.

   ○ Set the options for your plan.

       □ **Hard Disk:** Set the time for the hard disk to turn off when idle.

       □ **Wireless Adapter Settings:** Adjust power-saving mode for Wi-Fi.

       □ **USB Settings:** Control USB selective suspend to save energy.

       □ **Processor Power Management:**

          □ Minimum processor state: Set a percentage of the CPU's minimum power usage.

          □ Maximum processor state: Set the maximum CPU usage allowed.

       □ **Sleep:** Configure hibernation settings or allow wake timers.

       □ **Display:** Adjust screen brightness and turn-off times.

       □ **Battery (for laptops):** Set low, critical, and reserve battery levels and actions.

5. Activate Your Custom Plan:

   o Ensure your custom plan is selected in the Power Options menu.

How do I troubleshoot a printer in windows 11?

Printers can sometimes be challenging to troubleshoot, whether they fail to connect, print, or respond. Here are a few tips to help you diagnose and resolve most common printer problems.

Check Printer Connections

Before diving into software troubleshooting, ensure your printer's is connected and powered on.

- **Power Connection**: Make sure the printer is properly plugged into a working power outlet and turned **on**. Look for indicator lights on the printer.

- **USB Cable (Wired Printers)**: Check the USB cable is securely connected to both the printer and your computer. If available, try using a different USB cable or port.

- **Wi-Fi/Network Connection (Wireless Printers)**:

   o Confirm your printer is connected to the same **Wi-Fi network** as your computer.

   o Check your printer's display panel for Wi-Fi status or errors.

   o Restart your router and printer to refresh the network connection.

   o For network printers, you may also need to ensure the printer's **IP address** is properly set up.

   o Refer to your printer's manual for instructions on reconnecting to Wi-Fi if needed.

Select the Correct Printer

If you have multiple printers installed, the wrong one might be selected:

1. Open the document, photo, or webpage you want to print.

2. Press **Ctrl + P** (or look for the Print option in the application's menu).

3. In the Print window, locate the Printer dropdown or list.

4. Select the correct printer from the list of available printers.

5. Adjust any print settings (e.g., paper size, orientation).

Check Printer Status and Paper

- Ensure there is enough paper in the printer tray.

- Check for paper jams and clear them.

- Verify ink or toner levels; replace cartridges if needed.

- Restart the printer to clear any internal errors.

Check if Printer is Paused

Sometimes the printer pauses itself, to check

1. Press Windows + I to open **Settings**.

2. Go to **Bluetooth & devices > Printers & scanners**.

3. Click on the printer you are using.

4. Select **Open print queue**.

5. In the print queue window, next to the printer, click on the three dots on the right hand side.

6. From the drop down menu, select **Resume All.**

Clear the Print Queue

A stuck print job can block other documents from printing. To clear the queue:

1. Open **Settings > Bluetooth & devices > Printers & scanners**.

2. Click on your printer and select **Open print queue**.

3. Right-click on any stuck jobs and select **Cancel**.

4. Restart the printer and try printing again.

Restart Print Spooler Service

The **Print Spooler** manages print jobs sent to the printer. Restarting it can fix issues:

1. Press Windows + R, type services.msc, and press **Enter**.

2. In the Services list, find **Print Spooler**.

3. Right-click it and select **Restart**.

Chapter 2: Settings & Personalization

4. Close the window and check the printer again.

Reinstall Printer Driver

To reinstall the printer driver, first uninstall the current printer driver:

1. Open **Settings** by pressing Windows + I.

2. Go to **Bluetooth & devices** > **Printers & scanners**.

3. Find your printer in the list, click on it, and select **Remove device**.

4. Confirm the removal when prompted.

5. Go to the **manufacturer's support website** (e.g., HP, Canon, Epson, Brother).

6. Search for your printer model.

7. Download the latest driver software for **Windows 11** or **Windows 10** (64-bit).

8. Run the downloaded installer and follow the on-screen instructions.

Consult Manufacturer Support

If none of the above steps resolve the issue:

- Visit your printer manufacturer's support website.

    o **HP**: support.hp.com

    o **Canon**: usa.canon.com

    o **Epson**: epson.com/support

- Search for solutions specific to your printer model.

- Check for firmware updates or hardware issues.

3

Connectivity

Chapter 3: Connectivity

How Do I Connect to a Wi-Fi Network in Windows 11?

You can quickly scan for available networks, select your desired Wi-Fi connection, and enter the necessary credentials to establish a secure and reliable connection.

1. **Access Wi-Fi Settings:**

   o   Click on the **Network** icon located in the taskbar at the bottom right corner of your screen.

2. **View Available Networks:**

   o   A list of available Wi-Fi networks will appear. Scroll through to find the network you wish to connect to.

3. **Select and Connect:**

   o   Click on your desired Wi-Fi network.

   o   If it's a secure network, enter the **password** when prompted.

   o   Click **Connect**. You can also choose to **Connect automatically** for future connections.

4. **Confirm Connection:**

   o   Once connected, the network name will display as **Connected** with a signal strength indicator.

Additional Tips:

☐ **Manage Known Networks:**

　　o　Go to **Settings** > **Network & Internet** > **Wi-Fi** > **Manage known networks** to view, prioritize, or forget saved networks.

☐ **Toggle Wi-Fi On/Off:**

　　o　Use the Wi-Fi toggle in the **Network** menu or via **Settings** to enable or disable your Wi-Fi adapter.

How Do I Create a Mobile Hotspot in Windows 11?

Setting up a mobile hotspot allows you to share your internet connection with other devices, such as a smartphone, tablet, or another computer.

1. **Open Settings:**

　　o　Press **Windows + I** to open the **Settings** app.

2. **Navigate to Mobile Hotspot:**

　　o　Go to **Network & Internet** > **Mobile hotspot**.

3. **Configure Hotspot Settings:**

　　o　**Share my Internet connection from:** Choose the internet connection you want to share (e.g., Wi-Fi or Ethernet).

　　o　**Network name and password:** Click **Edit** to set a custom **Network name**, **Network password**, and **Network band** (2.4 GHz or 5 GHz).

4. **Enable Mobile Hotspot:**

　　o　Toggle the **Mobile hotspot** switch to **On**.

5. **Connect Devices:**

　　o　On your other devices, search for the newly created Wi-Fi network using the **Network name** and enter the **password** to connect.

Additional Tips:

☐ **Power Sharing:**

　　o　You can choose to share your connection via **Wi-Fi**, **Bluetooth**, or both.

Chapter 3: Connectivity

☐ **Data Usage:**

   o   Monitor the data usage of connected devices under the **Mobile hotspot** settings.

How do I connect to a Mobile Hotspot?

Connecting your Windows 11 PC to a mobile hotspot allows you to access the internet on the go, especially when traditional Wi-Fi networks are unavailable. You can connect to a hotspot created on an iPhone or Android Phone.

Enable your Mobile Hotspot

Before connecting your PC, make sure that the device you're using as a hotspot (e.g., smartphone) has its hotspot feature turned on.

For Android Devices:

1. **Open Settings:**

   o   Swipe down from the top of the screen and tap the **Settings** gear icon, or find **Settings** in your app drawer.

2. **Navigate to Hotspot Settings:**

   o   Go to **Network & Internet** > **Hotspot & tethering** > **Wi-Fi hotspot**.

3. **Activate the Hotspot:**

   o   Toggle the **Wi-Fi hotspot** switch to **On**.

   o   Note the **Network name (SSID)** and **Password** displayed. You can tap **Set up Wi-Fi hotspot** to customize these details.

For iOS Devices (iPhone/iPad):

1. **Open Settings:**

   o   Tap the **Settings** app on your home screen.

2. **Navigate to Personal Hotspot:**

   o   Go to **Personal Hotspot**.

3. **Activate the Hotspot:**

   o   Toggle **Allow Others to Join** to **On**.

o Note the **Wi-Fi Password**. You can tap the password field to change it if needed.

Connect Your Windows 11 PC to the Mobile Hotspot

Now, let's connect your Windows 11 PC to the active mobile hotspot.

1. **Access Network Settings:**

   o **Click on the Network icon** in the taskbar's lower-right corner. It typically looks like a Wi-Fi signal, Ethernet cable, or airplane mode icon.

2. **View Available Networks:**

   o A list of available Wi-Fi networks will appear.

3. **Select Your Hotspot:**

   o Find and **click on the SSID (network name)** of your mobile hotspot.

4. **Connect to the Hotspot:**

   o Click **"Connect"**.

5. **Enter the Password:**

   o Input the **Wi-Fi password** you noted earlier.

   o Optionally, check **"Connect automatically"** if you want your PC to reconnect to this hotspot whenever it's in range.

6. **Finalize the Connection:**

   o Click **"Next"**.

Wait for the connection to establish. You should see a confirmation once connected.

How Do I Set Up a Virtual Private Network (VPN)?

Setting up a Virtual Private Network (VPN) on Windows 11 enhances your online privacy and security by encrypting your internet connection and masking your IP address. Whether you're accessing sensitive information on public Wi-Fi, bypassing geo-restrictions, or ensuring a secure connection for remote work, configuring a VPN on your Windows 11 device is straightforward.

1. **Open Settings:**

o Press **Windows + I** to launch the **Settings** app.

2. **Navigate to VPN Settings:**

   o Go to **Network & Internet** > **VPN**.

3. **Add a VPN Connection:**

   o Click on **Add VPN**.

4. **Enter VPN Details:**

   o **VPN provider:** Select **Windows (built-in)**.

   o **Connection name:** Enter a name for the VPN connection (e.g., "Work VPN").

   o **Server name or address:** Enter the VPN server address provided by your VPN service.

   o **VPN type:** Choose the appropriate VPN protocol (e.g., **L2TP/IPsec**, **PPTP**, **SSTP**, **IKEv2**).

   o **Type of sign-in info:** Select the authentication method (e.g., **Username and password**).

5. **Save the VPN Connection:**

   o After filling in all details, click **Save**.

6. **Connect to the VPN:**

   o Back in the **VPN** settings, select the VPN connection you created and click **Connect**.

   o Enter your **username** and **password** if prompted.

Additional Tips:

☐ **Manage VPN Connections:**

   o Edit or remove VPN connections from the **VPN** settings page as needed.

☐ **Third-Party VPN Clients:**

   o Alternatively, you can use VPN applications provided by third-party VPN services for additional features and ease of use. For example:

   ExpressVPN, NordVPN, CyberGhost, Surfshark, Private Internet Access (PIA), ProtonVPN, Windscribe, Hotspot Shield, TunnelBear, and IPVanish.

How Do I Manage Network Adapters in Windows 11?

A network adapter (also known as a network interface card or NIC) is a hardware component that allows your computer to communicate over a network. This can be through wired connections like Ethernet or wireless connections like Wi-Fi.

1. **Open Network Connections:**

   o   Press **Windows + R**, type ncpa.cpl, and press **Enter**.

2. **View Network Adapters:**

   o   You'll see a list of all network adapters, including **Wi-Fi**, **Ethernet**, **Bluetooth**, and virtual adapters.

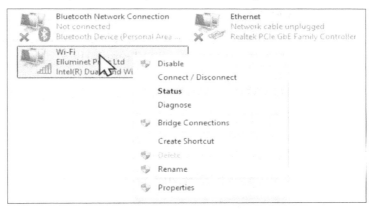

3. **Enable or Disable Adapters:**

   o   **Disable an Adapter:**

       ☐ Right-click the desired adapter and select **Disable**.

   o   **Enable an Adapter:**

       ☐ Right-click a disabled adapter and select **Enable**.

4. **Rename Adapters (Optional):**

   o   Right-click an adapter, select **Rename**, and enter a new name for easier identification.

5. **Access Adapter Properties:**

   o   Right-click an adapter and choose **Properties** to configure settings like IPv4, IPv6, client protocols, and more.

6. Install or Update Drivers:

- o Right-click an adapter and select **Update driver** to install the latest drivers.

- o To install a new driver, choose **Update driver** > **Browse my computer for drivers**.

Additional Tips:

- ☐ **Troubleshooting Connectivity:**

  - o Access **Device Manager** by pressing **Windows + X** and selecting **Device Manager** for more detailed adapter management.

- ☐ **Virtual Adapters:**

  - o Virtual adapters created by VPNs or virtual machines can also be managed similarly.

How Do I Prioritize Wi-Fi Networks in Windows 11?

Windows 11 does not provide a direct interface to prioritize Wi-Fi networks through the Settings app. However, you can manage the priority of Wi-Fi networks using the Command Prompt. Here's how:

1. Open Command Prompt as Administrator:

- o Press **Windows + X** and select **Windows Terminal (Admin)** or **Command Prompt (Admin)**.

2. View Preferred Networks:

- o Type the following command and press **Enter**:

- o `netsh wlan show profiles`

- o This will display a list of all saved Wi-Fi profiles.

3. Set Priority for a Network:

- o To set the priority of a specific network, use the following command:

- o `netsh wlan set profileorder name="ProfileName" interface="Wi-Fi" priority=1`

- o Replace "ProfileName" with the exact name of your Wi-Fi network.

o   The priority value determines the order (1 is the highest priority).

4. Repeat for Other Networks:

o   Assign priority values to other networks as needed, ensuring no two networks have the same priority number.

5. Verify Changes:

o   Run `netsh wlan show profiles` again to confirm the updated order.

Alternative Method:

☐   **Forget and Reconnect:**

o   Windows tends to prioritize networks based on the order they were connected. By forgetting less preferred networks and reconnecting to your preferred one first, you can influence the priority.

Additional Tips:

☐   **Automate Priority Settings:**

o   Consider creating a script with the necessary netsh commands to automate network prioritization if you frequently change networks.

☐   **Third-Party Tools:**

o   Some third-party applications offer user-friendly interfaces for managing Wi-Fi network priorities.

How Do I Set Up a Network Bridge in Windows 11?

Setting up a Network Bridge allows you to connect two or more network segments, enabling devices on different networks to communicate as if they were on the same local network. This can be particularly useful in scenarios where you want to share an internet connection from one network adapter to another or integrate wired and wireless networks seamlessly.

A network bridge allows you to connect two or more network segments, making them function as a single network.

1. Open Network Connections:

o   Press **Windows + R**, type ncpa.cpl, and press **Enter**.

2. **Select Adapters to Bridge:**

   o Hold down the **Ctrl** key and click on the network adapters you want to bridge (e.g., Ethernet and Wi-Fi).

3. **Create Bridge:**

   o Right-click on one of the selected adapters and choose **Bridge Connections**.

   o Windows will create a new network bridge, and the selected adapters will be part of this bridge.

4. **Verify Bridge Creation:**

   o A new **Network Bridge** icon will appear in the Network Connections window, indicating that the bridge is active.

Additional Tips:

☐ **Removing a Bridge:**

   o To remove the bridge, right-click on the **Network Bridge** icon and select **Delete** or **Remove**.

☐ **Compatibility:**

   o Ensure that the network adapters you intend to bridge are compatible and properly configured for bridging.

☐ **Use Cases:**

   o Network bridges can be useful for connecting different network types or extending network segments without additional hardware.

How Do I Configure Proxy Settings in Windows 11?

Setting up a proxy server can enhance your network's security, improve performance, and provide greater control over internet usage. Whether you're aiming to anonymize your browsing, filter content, or cache data for faster access, a proxy server serves as an intermediary between your device and the internet.

1. **Open Settings:**

   o Press **Windows + I** to launch the **Settings** app.

2. **Navigate to Proxy Settings:**

   o Go to **Network & Internet** > **Proxy**.

3. **Set Up a Proxy Server:**

   o **Automatic Proxy Setup:**

      ☐ **Automatically detect settings:** Toggle **On** to allow Windows to automatically detect proxy settings.

      ☐ **Use setup script:** If provided, enter the script address and toggle **On**.

   o **Manual Proxy Setup:**

      ☐ Toggle **Use a proxy server** to **On**.

      ☐ Enter the **Address** and **Port** of the proxy server.

      ☐ Optionally, check **Don't use proxy server for local (intranet) addresses**.

      ☐ Click **Save** to apply the settings.

4. **Disable Proxy (If Needed):**

   o Toggle **Use a proxy server** to **Off** to disable manual proxy settings.

Additional Tips:

☐ **Proxy Authentication:**

   o If your proxy requires authentication, you may need to enter your **username** and **password** when prompted by applications.

☐ **Browser-Specific Settings:**

   o Some browsers (like Firefox) have their own proxy settings independent of Windows. Ensure consistency across applications if needed.

☐ **Security Considerations:**

   o Use trusted proxy servers to protect your data and privacy.

How Do I View Network Usage in Windows 11?

Monitoring your network usage in shows how your system uses internet resources, and allows you to identify bandwidth-heavy applications, and ensure optimal performance. This is useful for troubleshooting connectivity issues, or managing data consumption.

Chapter 3: Connectivity

1. **Open Task Manager:**

   o Press **Ctrl + Shift + Esc** to open **Task Manager**.

   o Alternatively, right-click the taskbar and select **Task Manager**.

2. **Navigate to the Performance Tab:**

   o Click on the **Performance** tab at the top.

3. **Select Network:**

   o On the left sidebar, select **Wi-Fi** or **Ethernet** depending on your connection type.

4. **View Network Activity:**

   o Here, you can see real-time data on **Send**, **Receive**, **Link Speed**, **Data Usage**, and more.

   o **Graphs** display current network utilization.

5. **Detailed Network Usage:**

   o For a more detailed view, go back to **Task Manager**.

   o Click on the **Processes** tab.

   o Under the **Network** column, you can see the network usage per application.

Alternative Method:

❑ **Settings App:**

1. Open **Settings** by pressing **Windows + I**.

2. Go to **Network & Internet** > **Data usage**.

3. Select your active network to view data consumption by apps over different time periods.

Additional Tips:

❑ **Data Limits:** Set data limits in **Data usage** settings to monitor and manage your data consumption effectively.

❑ **Background Processes:** Identify applications with high network usage in **Task Manager** to manage bandwidth allocation.

How Do I Enable or Disable Wi-Fi on Windows 11?

1. **Using the Taskbar:**

   o   Click on the **Network** icon in the taskbar.

   o   Toggle the **Wi-Fi** switch to **On** or **Off** as desired.

2. **Through Settings:**

   o   Press **Windows + I** to open the **Settings** app.

   o   Go to **Network & Internet** > **Wi-Fi**.

   o   Toggle the **Wi-Fi** switch to **On** or **Off**.

3. **Using Keyboard Shortcuts (If Available):**

   o   Some laptops have a dedicated **Wi-Fi** toggle key (e.g., **Fn + F12**). Refer to your laptop's manual for specific shortcuts.

4. **Via Airplane Mode:**

   o   Click on the **Network** icon in the taskbar.

   o   Toggle **Airplane Mode** to **On** to disable all wireless communications, including Wi-Fi.

   o   Toggle **Off** to re-enable Wi-Fi and other wireless connections.

Additional Tips:

☐   **Hardware Switch:** Some desktops and laptops come with a physical Wi-Fi switch. Ensure it's turned on if available.

☐   **Power Management:** To prevent Windows from turning off your Wi-Fi adapter to save power:

   1. Open **Device Manager** by pressing **Windows + X** and selecting **Device Manager**.

   2. Expand **Network adapters**, right-click your **Wi-Fi adapter**, and select **Properties**.

   3. Go to the **Power Management** tab.

   4. Uncheck **Allow the computer to turn off this device to save power**.

   5. Click **OK** to apply changes.

Chapter 3: Connectivity

How Do I View Connected Devices on My PC?

Windows 11 provides several built-in tools that allow you to easily identify and manage all hardware and networked devices currently linked to your computer.

1. **For Bluetooth and Peripheral Devices:**

    o **Open Settings:**

        □ Press **Windows + I** to open **Settings**.

    o **Navigate to Bluetooth & Devices:**

        □ Go to **Bluetooth & devices**.

    o **View Connected Devices:**

        □ Under **Devices**, you'll see a list of connected Bluetooth devices, printers, and other peripherals.

        □ Click on a specific device to view more details or manage its settings.

2. **For Network Devices:**

    o **Open Settings:**

        □ Press **Windows + I** to access **Settings**.

    o **Go to Network Status:**

        □ Navigate to **Network & Internet** > **Advanced network settings** > **More network adapter options**.

    o **View Network Adapters:**

        □ Here, you can see all network adapters and their connection statuses.

        □ Double-click an adapter to view its status, including connected devices if applicable.

3. **Using Device Manager:**

    o **Open Device Manager:**

        □ Press **Windows + X** and select **Device Manager**.

    o **Browse Devices:**

☐ Expand categories like **Network adapters**, **Bluetooth**, **Printers**, etc., to view connected devices.

o **Check Device Status:**

☐ Right-click on a device and select **Properties** to view more information.

4. **Using Command Prompt for Network Devices:**

o **Open Command Prompt:**

☐ Press **Windows + R**, type cmd, and press **Enter**.

o **List Connected Devices:**

☐ Type the following command and press **Enter**:

☐ arp -a

☐ This will display a list of devices connected to your network with their IP and MAC addresses.

Additional Tips:

☐ **Third-Party Applications:**

o Use network monitoring tools like **Advanced IP Scanner** or **Wireless Network Watcher** for a more comprehensive view of connected devices.

☐ **Router Interface:**

o Access your router's admin panel (usually via a web browser) to see all devices connected to your network, including their IP and MAC addresses.

How Do I Change My DNS Settings in Windows 11?

Changing your DNS (Domain Name System) settings allows you to specify which servers your computer uses to translate website domain names into IP addresses.

1. **Open Settings:**

o Press **Windows + I** to launch the **Settings** app.

2. **Navigate to Network Settings:**

o Go to **Network & Internet**

3. **Select your network Adapter**

   - o   For Ethernet, select Ethernet

   - o   For Wi-Fi, select **Wi-Fi**, then select **properties.**

4. Click **Edit** under **DNS Server Assignment** to set DNS Server IP addresses:

   - o   Set DNS from automatic to manual using the drop down box at the top of the window.

   - o   Turn on IPv4

   - o   In preferred DNS, enter your primary DNS server IP Address. In alternative DNS, enter your secondary DNS server IP address

   - o   Alternatively, you can use other public DNS services such as

       - ☐   **Cloudflare** (1.1.1.1 and 1.0.0.1)

       - ☐   **OpenDNS** (208.67.222.222 and 208.67.220.220)

       - ☐   **GoogleDNS** (8.8.8.8 and 8.8.4.4)

5. **Save Changes:**

   - o   Click **Save** to apply the settings.

6. **Flush DNS Cache (Optional):**

   - o   Open **Command Prompt** by pressing **Windows + R**, typing cmd, and pressing **Enter**.

   - o   Type the following command and press **Enter**:

     ```
     ipconfig /flushdns
     ```

   - o   This clears the DNS cache to ensure the new settings take effect immediately.

Additional Tips:

☐   **IPv6 DNS:**

   - o   To set DNS servers for IPv6, repeat the above steps for **Internet Protocol Version 6 (TCP/IPv6)**.

☐   **Testing DNS Changes:**

o Use websites like **DNS Leak Test** to verify that your DNS settings are correctly configured.

☐ **Benefits of Changing DNS:**

o Improved browsing speed, enhanced security, and access to region-restricted content.

How do I use DNS over HTTPs (DoH)?

DNS (Domain Name System) translates human-readable domain names (like www.example.com) into IP addresses that computers use to identify each other on the network. Traditionally, DNS queries are sent over unencrypted channels, making them vulnerable to eavesdropping and manipulation

DNS over HTTPS (DoH) works by encrypting DNS queries using the HTTPS protocol. This encryption ensures that DNS requests and responses are secure from interception and tampering. This protects against DNS spoofing and man-in-the-middle attacks by ensuring the integrity and authenticity of DNS responses.

Windows 11 includes built-in support for DNS over HTTPS. You can enable it as follows:

1. **Open Settings:**

   o Press **Windows + I** to launch the **Settings** app.

2. **Navigate to Network Settings:**

   o Go to **Network & Internet**

3. **Select your network Adapter**

   o For Ethernet, select Ethernet

   o For Wi-Fi, select **Wi-Fi**, then select **properties.**

4. Click **Edit** under **DNS Server Assignment**

5. Enable DNS over HTTPS:

   o Select **On (manual template)**

6. Enter Server URLs in **DNS over HTTPS Template**

   o Cloudflare General DNS:
   `https://cloudflare-dns.com/dns-query`

   o Cloudflare Family Filter DNS:

> `https://family.cloudflare-dns.com/dns-query`

- o Google Public DNS:
  `https://dns.google/dns-query`

- o OpenDNS:
  `https://doh.opendns.com/dns-query`

7. **Save Changes:**

   - o Click **Save** to apply the settings.

8. **Flush DNS Cache (Optional):**

   - o Open **Command Prompt** by pressing **Windows + R**, typing cmd, and pressing **Enter**.

   - o Type the following command and press **Enter**:

     `ipconfig /flushdns`

   - o This clears the DNS cache to ensure the new settings take effect immediately.

How Do I Disable Proxy Settings in Windows 11?

1. **Open Settings:**

   - o Press **Windows + I** to access the **Settings** app.

2. **Navigate to Proxy Settings:**

   - o Go to **Network & Internet** > **Proxy**.

3. **Disable Manual Proxy Setup:**

   - o Under **Manual proxy setup**, toggle **Use a proxy server** to **Off**.

4. **Disable Automatic Proxy Setup (If Needed):**

   - o Under **Automatic proxy setup**, toggle **Automatically detect settings** to **Off** if you do not want Windows to automatically detect proxy settings.

5. **Save Changes:**

   - o Changes are saved automatically. Close the **Settings** window.

Additional Tips:

▢ **Browser-Specific Proxy Settings:**

    o   Some browsers have their own proxy settings. Ensure that proxy configurations are disabled within your browser if needed.

▢ **VPN and Proxy Conflicts:**

    o   If you're using a VPN, ensure that proxy settings do not conflict with your VPN connection for optimal performance.

How Do I Use the Windows 11 Network Troubleshooter?

While the focus is not on troubleshooting, understanding how to access built-in tools can enhance your connectivity experience. Here's how to access and use the Network Troubleshooter in Windows 11:

1. **Open Settings:**

    o   Press **Windows + I** to open the **Settings** app.

2. **Navigate to Troubleshoot:**

    o   Go to **System** > **Troubleshoot** > **Other troubleshooters**.

3. **Run the Network Troubleshooter:**

    o   Under **Most frequent**, find **Network Adapter**.

    o   Click **Run** next to it.

4. **Follow On-Screen Instructions:**

    o   The troubleshooter will guide you through steps to identify and fix network-related issues.

    o   Follow the prompts to complete the process.

Additional Tips:

▢ **Multiple Troubleshooters:**

    o   Explore other troubleshooters under **Other troubleshooters** for different network components, such as **Internet Connections**, **Incoming Connections**, etc.

▢ **Automatic Fixes:**

    o   The Network Troubleshooter can automatically detect and apply fixes for common connectivity problems.

Chapter 3: Connectivity

How Do I View and Manage My Network Profiles?

Managing your network profiles in Windows 11 is crucial for controlling how your PC interacts with different networks. Network profiles, such as Public, Private, and Domain, determine the security settings and accessibility of your device on each network. By viewing and adjusting these profiles, you can enhance your system's security, manage network discoverability, and ensure appropriate access permissions based on the environment you are connected to.

1. **Open Settings:**

   o   Press **Windows + I** to launch the **Settings** app.

2. **Navigate to Network Profiles:**

   o   Go to **Network & Internet**.

   o   Click on **Wi-Fi** or **Ethernet** depending on your connection type.

3. **View Connected Network:**

   o   Under your active connection, click on the network name to view its properties.

4. **Set Network as Public or Private:**

   o   **Public Network:**

      ☐   Choose this option if you're connected to a public hotspot or a network in a public place. It offers stricter security settings.

   o   **Private Network:**

      ☐   Select this if you're on a trusted network, like your home or office. It allows for device discovery and file sharing.

5. **Change Network Profile:**

   o   Click on **Properties** under the network name.

   o   Under **Network profile**, select either **Public** or **Private** based on your preference.

6. **Manage Network Discovery and Sharing:**

   o   For **Private Networks**, ensure **Network discovery** and **File and printer sharing** are enabled if you want to share resources.

o For **Public Networks**, these options are typically disabled to enhance security.

Additional Tips:

☐ **Multiple Network Profiles:**

o Each Wi-Fi network you connect to can have its own profile settings, allowing for customized security and sharing options.

☐ **Viewing All Profiles via Command Prompt:**

o Open **Command Prompt** and type netsh wlan show profiles to view all saved Wi-Fi profiles on your PC.

How Do I Set Up a Wired Ethernet Connection?

Establishing a wired Ethernet connection in Windows 11 provides a reliable and high-speed internet connection by directly linking your PC to a router or modem using an Ethernet cable. This setup can enhance network stability, reduce latency, and improve overall performance compared to wireless connections.

1. **Connect the Ethernet Cable:**

o Plug one end of the Ethernet cable into your PC's Ethernet port and the other end into your router or modem.

2. **Automatic Detection:**

o Windows 11 should automatically detect the wired connection and establish it without additional setup.

3. **Verify Connection:**

o Click on the **Network** icon in the taskbar.

o Ensure that the **Ethernet** connection shows as **Connected**.

4. **Configure Ethernet Settings (Optional):**

o **Open Settings:**

☐ Press **Windows + I** to access **Settings**.

o **Navigate to Ethernet Settings:**

☐ Go to **Network & Internet** > **Ethernet**.

o **View Connection Details:**

☐ Click on your Ethernet connection to view properties like IP address, DNS servers, and more.

o **Set IP Configuration:**

☐ Under **Edit IP assignment**, you can set a static IP address or ensure it's set to **Automatic (DHCP)**.

5. **Troubleshoot if Necessary:**

o If the connection isn't established, ensure the Ethernet cable is securely connected and the router/modem is functioning properly.

Additional Tips:

☐ **Network Speed:**

o Wired connections generally offer more stable and faster internet speeds compared to wireless connections.

☐ **Adapter Settings:**

o Manage Ethernet adapter settings via **Device Manager** for advanced configurations or driver updates.

How Do I Create a Network Map in Windows 11?

Creating a network map helps visualize devices and connections within your network. While Windows 11 doesn't have a built-in network mapping tool like some previous versions, you can use third-party applications or utilize built-in network discovery features.

Using Network Discovery:

1. **Enable Network Discovery:**

o Open **Settings** by pressing **Windows + I**.

o Go to **Network & Internet** > **Wi-Fi** or **Ethernet** > **Properties**.

o Under **Network profile**, ensure **Private** is selected to enable network discovery.

2. **Access Network in File Explorer:**

   o   Open **File Explorer** by pressing **Windows + E**.

   o   Click on **Network** in the left sidebar.

   o   Windows will scan and display devices connected to your network.

3. **View Device Information:**

   o   Click on individual devices to see shared folders and other accessible resources.

Using Third-Party Software:

☐   **Microsoft Visio:**

   o   Create detailed network diagrams using Visio's templates and shapes.

☐   **Advanced IP Scanner:**

   o   Scan your network to identify all connected devices and visualize their connections.

☐   **Lucidchart or Draw.io:**

   o   Online tools that offer customizable network mapping features.

Additional Tips:

☐   **Security Considerations:**

   o   Ensure that network discovery is enabled only on trusted networks to prevent unauthorized access.

☐   **Regular Updates:**

   o   Keep your network map updated by periodically scanning for new or removed devices.

How Do I Set Up a Guest Network in Windows 11?

Setting up a guest network allows visitors to access the internet without giving them access to your main network resources. This feature is managed through your router rather than directly through Windows 11. This is a general guide, consult your router's instructions for specific details.

Chapter 3: Connectivity

1. **Access Your Router's Admin Panel:**

   o Open a web browser and enter your router's IP address (commonly 192.168.1.1 or 192.168.0.1).

   o Log in using your **admin username** and **password**. Refer to your router's manual if you're unsure.

2. **Navigate to Guest Network Settings:**

   o Look for sections labeled **Guest Network**, **Wireless Settings**, or **Network Settings**.

3. **Enable Guest Network:**

   o Toggle the **Guest Network** feature to **On**.

4. **Configure Guest Network Details:**

   o **Network Name (SSID):** Assign a unique name to distinguish it from your main network.

   o **Security Type:** Choose **WPA2-Personal** or a higher security standard.

   o **Password:** Set a strong password for guests to connect.

5. **Set Access Permissions:**

   o Restrict guest access to the internet only, preventing access to your main network's devices and shared resources.

6. **Save and Apply Settings:**

   o Click **Save** or **Apply** to activate the guest network.

7. **Connect Devices to Guest Network:**

   o Guests can now connect using the **Guest Network SSID** and **password** you provided.

Additional Tips:

☐ **Separate Bandwidth:** Some routers allow you to allocate specific bandwidth limits to guest networks to ensure your main network's performance isn't affected.

☐ **Guest Network Visibility:** Decide whether the guest network should be visible to devices or hidden for added security.

☐ **Periodic Password Changes:** Regularly update the guest network password to maintain security.

How Do I Use AirDrop Alternatives for Windows 11?

While AirDrop is exclusive to Apple devices, Windows 11 offers several alternatives for seamless file sharing between devices:

1. **Nearby Sharing:**

   o **Enable Nearby Sharing:**

      ☐ Open **Settings** > **System** > **Shared experiences**.

      ☐ Toggle **Nearby sharing** to **On**.

      ☐ Choose to share content with **Everyone nearby** or **My devices only**.

   o **Share Files:**

      ☐ Right-click the file you want to share and select **Share**.

      ☐ Choose the nearby device from the list to send the file.

2. **Bluetooth File Transfer:**

   o **Pair Devices:**

      ☐ Ensure both devices have Bluetooth enabled and are paired.

   o **Send Files:**

      ☐ Right-click the file, select **Send to** > **Bluetooth device**, and choose the recipient device.

3. **OneDrive:**

   o **Upload Files:**

      ☐ Save files to your **OneDrive** account.

   o **Access Files:**

      ☐ Other devices can access shared files via the OneDrive app or website.

How Do I Monitor My Network Traffic in Windows 11?

Monitoring network traffic helps you understand how data is being used on your PC.

Chapter 3: Connectivity

There are several ways to do this, including using Task Manager.

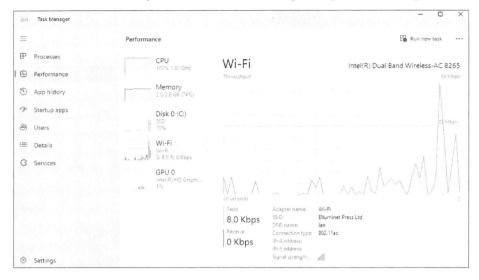

1. **Using Task Manager:**

   o **Open Task Manager:**

      □ Press **Ctrl + Shift + Esc** to open **Task Manager**.

   o **Go to the Performance Tab:**

      □ Click on **Performance**.

      □ Select **Wi-Fi** or **Ethernet** to view real-time data usage and network performance metrics.

   o **Processes Tab:**

      □ Under the **Processes** tab, you can see which applications are using the network under the **Network** column.

2. **Using Resource Monitor:**

   o **Open Resource Monitor:**

      □ Press **Windows + R**, type resmon, and press **Enter**.

   o **Navigate to the Network Tab:**

      □ Click on the **Network** tab to view detailed information about network activity, including processes with network activity, TCP connections, and network utilization.

3. **Using Third-Party Tools:**

   o **GlassWire:**

      ☐ Offers detailed network monitoring, data usage tracking, and alerts for unusual activity.

      `www.glasswire.com /download/`

   o **NetLimiter:**

      ☐ Allows you to monitor and control the bandwidth usage of applications.

      `www.netlimiter.com`

   o **Wireshark:**

      ☐ A powerful network protocol analyzer for in-depth network traffic analysis.

      `www.wireshark.org`

4. **Using Windows Settings:**

   o **View Data Usage:**

      ☐ Open **Settings** > **Network & Internet** > **Data usage** to see how much data each application has consumed over a specific period.

How Do I Change the Default Web Browser

Changing the default web browser allows you to choose your preferred browser for opening web links and browsing the internet.

1. **Open Settings:**

   o Press **Win + I** to open **Settings**.

   o Navigate to **Apps** > **Default apps**.

2. **Select Your Preferred Browser:**

   o Scroll through the list or use the search bar to find your preferred web browser (e.g., **Google Chrome**, **Mozilla Firefox**, **Microsoft Edge**).

3. Set as Default:

- o   Click on the browser's name.

- o   You'll see a list of file types and link types (e.g., .htm, .html, HTTP, HTTPS).

- o   Click on each file or link type and select your preferred browser from the list.

- o   Repeat this for all relevant file and link types to ensure comprehensive default settings.

4. Confirm Changes:

- o   After setting your preferred browser for all relevant file and link types, close the Settings app.

Additional Tips:

- **Install New Browsers:** If your preferred browser isn't listed, ensure it's installed on your system. Download it from the official website.

- **Use a Single Browser:** To avoid confusion, ensure that all relevant file and link types are associated with your preferred browser.

- **Manage Browser Extensions:** Customize your browser with extensions to enhance functionality and security based on your needs.

How do I troubleshoot internet connectivity issues?

Internet connection failures can occur due to a wide range of factors, such as hardware malfunctions, software misconfigurations, or external influences such as service outages or interference.

These issues may be caused by the modem or router, or by improper settings and configuration. Environmental factors, such as interference or physical obstructions, can also weaken wireless signals. Additionally, external causes, including ISP outages or network congestion, may be causing the issue.

Here are a few things you can try.

Check your Wi-Fi or Ethernet Connection

- **For Wi-Fi**:

    1. Click the **Network icon** in the taskbar (bottom-right corner).

    2. Check if Wi-Fi is turned on. If it's off, click the Wi-Fi button to enable it.

    3. Look for your network in the available list and select it. If prompted, enter the password to connect.

- **For Ethernet**:

    1. Confirm that the Ethernet cable is securely plugged into your PC and router or modem.

    2. Inspect the Ethernet port on your computer. A green or amber light usually indicates a proper connection.

Check Airplane Mode

Sometimes, Airplane Mode can inadvertently disable all network connections.

1. Press **Windows + A** to open **Quick Settings**.

2. Look for the **Airplane Mode** icon. If it's highlighted, click it to turn it off.

Try Restarting Your Devices

Restarting your devices can often resolve temporary glitches in network connectivity. This simple step resets hardware and software components, clearing up potential issues.

1. **Restart Your Router or Modem**:

    ☐ Turn off the device by unplugging it from the power source.

    ☐ Wait for at least 30 seconds before plugging it back in.

    ☐ Allow the router/modem a minute or two to reboot fully and connect to your ISP.

2. **Reconnect**:

    ☐ After restarting check if the internet connection is restored.

Chapter 3: Connectivity

Check Network Adapter Status

Your network adapter acts as the link between your computer and the internet. A disabled or malfunctioning adapter can cause connectivity problems.

1. Press **Windows + X** and select **Device Manager**.

2. Expand the **Network adapters** category.

3. Right-click your active network adapter (e.g., Wi-Fi or Ethernet). From the menu:

   ☐ Select **Enable Device** if it's disabled.

   ☐ Select **Properties** and check for any error messages under the **General** tab.

4. If there's a yellow warning triangle, it indicates a driver or hardware issue. Try reinstalling the driver.

   • Select the **Driver** tab.

   • Right-click on your active adapter and choose **Update driver**.

   • Select **Search automatically for drivers**.

   • If no updates are found, visit the manufacturer's website and download the latest driver.

Try Resetting IP and DNS Configurations

Misconfigured IP or DNS settings can block your connection to the internet. Resetting these can resolve many connectivity problems.

1. Open **Command Prompt** as Administrator:

   ☐ Press **Windows + X**, then select **Windows Terminal (Admin)**.

2. Type the following to release and renew your IP address:

   ```
   ipconfig /release
   ipconfig /renew
   ```

3. Flush the DNS cache to resolve domain name issues:

   ```
   ipconfig /flushdns
   ```

4. Restart your computer and check your connection.

Check Proxy Settings

Proxy settings can sometimes interfere with your connection, especially if they've been configured incorrectly or maliciously altered.

1. Press **Windows + I** to open **Settings**.

2. Navigate to **Network & Internet** > **Proxy**.

3. Ensure that **Use a proxy server** is turned off for **use setup script**, and **use a proxy server**, unless required by your work, college, or school network. If it is required, contact your network administrator.

Try Resetting Network Settings

A network reset restores all network-related settings to their defaults, which can resolve persistent issues.

1. Open **Settings**:

   ☐ Press **Windows + I**.

2. Go to **Network & Internet** > **Advanced network settings** > **Network reset**.

3. Click **Reset now** and confirm.

4. Restart your computer when prompted. You'll need to reconnect to Wi-Fi networks afterward.

Test Your Connection Using Command Prompt

Using Command Prompt can help you identify where the issue lies by testing your network's responsiveness.

1. Open **Command Prompt**:

   ☐ Press **Windows + X** and select **Windows Terminal**.

2. Test connectivity to a website. Type the following:

   ```
   ping google.com
   ```

3. Analyze the results:

   ☐ If you receive responses with time values (e.g., Reply from), your connection is working.

   ☐ If you see timeouts or no response, the issue might be with your network or ISP.

103

Check VPN settings (If you're using a VPN

1. Temporarily disconnect from your VPN to see if the connection improves.

2. If you rely on a VPN, switch to a different server to check if the issue is specific to the one you're connected to.

3. Ensure your VPN software is up to date, as outdated versions may cause connectivity issues.

4. Test Without VPN to see if the connection works. There may be an issue with the VPN provider.

Try Windows Network Troubleshooter

Windows 11 includes a built-in troubleshooter to detect and fix common network issues automatically. This tool is an excellent starting point for identifying problems without advanced technical knowledge.

1. Open **Settings**:

   ☐ Press **Windows + I**.

2. Navigate to **System** > **Troubleshoot** > **Other Troubleshooters**.

3. Locate **Internet Connections** in the list.

4. Click **Run** next to it.

5. Follow the on-screen instructions. The troubleshooter will attempt to identify and resolve the issue.

Check with your ISP or System Administrator for Issues

If all local troubleshooting steps fail, the problem might be with your internet service provider (ISP) or router.

1. **Test Other Devices**:

   ☐ Connect another device (e.g., a phone or tablet) to the same network.

   ☐ If the second device also fails to connect, the issue is likely with your ISP or router.

2. **Contact Your ISP**:

   ☐ Reach out to your ISP for support. They can run diagnostics and help identify outages or problems with your connection.

How do I share files over a local network?

Sharing files over a local network in Windows 11 allows you to transfer data between computers connected to the same network efficiently.

Step 1: Prepare the Network

Before sharing files, ensure all devices are connected to the same local network (Wi-Fi or Ethernet).

Verify Network Type

1. Press **Windows + I** to open **Settings**.

2. Go to **Network & Internet**.

3. Under your active connection (Wi-Fi or Ethernet), select properties

4. Ensure the network type is set to **Private**:

   o   Click on the connection name.

   o   Under **Network profile type**, select **Private**.

Enable Network Discovery

1. Open **Settings** > **Network & Internet**.

2. Scroll down and select **Advanced network settings** > **Advanced sharing settings**.

3. Under the **Private** network profile, enable:

   o   **Network discovery**.

   o   **File and printer sharing**.

Step 2: Share the Folder

You can share specific folders with other users on the network.

Locate the Folder

1. Open File explorer, find the folder you want to share.

2. Hold down shift, then right-click on the folder icon, then select **Properties**.

Configure Sharing Options

1. Go to the **Sharing** tab and click **Advanced Sharing**.

105

2. In the Advanced Sharing window, tick the box labeled **Share this folder**.

3. Set share folder name:

   o By default, the share name is the same as the folder name. You can change it by editing the Share name field

4. Configure Permissions

   o Click the **Permissions** button.

   o Enter the users or groups you want to share the folder with. Click **Add**, then enter usernames or email addresses.

      o In **Enter object names to select** field, type in the user's email address or username, then click **Check Names.** If the names don't show up click **Advanced**, then click **Find Now** to list all users and groups. Select the users you want from the list, click **OK**.

      Note, these users need to have user accounts on your computer or be part of your network domain. To add users to your computer, open the settings app, go to **Accounts > Other users,** click **Add account.** Follow the prompts.

      o Set the permission level (**Full Control**, **Change** or **Read**) for each user. **Change** permission is usually enough.

5. Click **OK** all windows, except the last one.

6. Take note of the network path in the shared properties dialog box. You'll need this to connect from another PC.

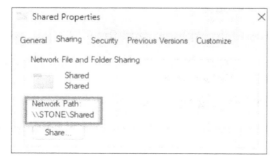

Step 3: Access Shared Files from Another Device

Other devices on the same network can now access the shared folder.

Access Using File Explorer

1. Open **File Explorer** on the other computer.

2. Type the network path you noted earlier into the address field at the top of the window.

3. You'll also find the computer you shared the folder from in the **Network** section on the side panel. Double-click the name of the computer sharing the folder.

4. Enter the username and password of the account on the computer sharing the folder .

5. When the folder opens, you can drag and drop files to add them or double-click existing files to open them.

How do I set up Bluetooth devices in Windows 11?

Setting up Bluetooth devices in Windows 11 is a straightforward process that allows you to connect peripherals such as headphones, keyboards, pens and mice.

Step 1: Turn On Bluetooth

Before pairing a device, ensure Bluetooth is enabled on your Windows 11 PC.

1. **Open Settings App**:

   o Press **Windows + I** to open the **Settings** app.

2. Navigate to **Devices** > **Bluetooth & devices**.

3. Toggle the **Bluetooth** switch to **On**.

Chapter 3: Connectivity

Step 2: Make the Device Discoverable

Most Bluetooth devices need to be in "pairing mode" to connect to your PC.

1. Refer to the device's user manual for instructions on how to enable pairing mode. Typically, this involves holding a specific button (e.g., a power or pairing button) until the device's indicator light blinks.

Step 3: Pair the Bluetooth Device

Once Bluetooth is enabled on your PC and the device is discoverable, proceed to pair the device.

1. **Open Settings App**:

   o Go to **Settings** > **Bluetooth & devices**.

2. Click **Add device**.

3. In the pop-up window, select **Bluetooth**.

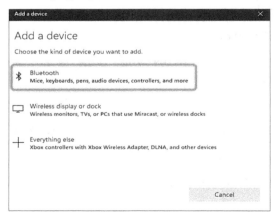

4. Windows will search for nearby devices. Select your device from the list.

5. Follow any on-screen prompts to complete the pairing process. For some devices, you may need to enter a PIN or confirm a passcode displayed on both devices.

6. Once paired, the device will appear at the top of the screen in the Bluetooth settings.

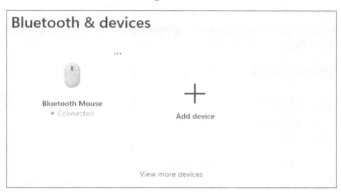

Step 4: Test the Device

To ensure the Bluetooth device is working:

1. **Audio Devices**:

   o Click the **Volume icon** in the taskbar and select the Bluetooth device as the audio output.

2. **Input Devices (Keyboards/Mice)**:

   o Test typing or cursor movement to confirm functionality.

3. **Other Devices**:

   o Use the device as intended and check for proper performance.

How do I enable/disable airplane mode?

Airplane mode is a feature that disables all wireless communication on your device with a single toggle.

It is designed to comply with aviation regulations that restrict the use of wireless signals during flights to avoid interference with aircraft systems.

Chapter 3: Connectivity

When airplane mode is enabled, the following are turned off:

1. **Wi-Fi**: Disconnects from all wireless internet networks.

2. **Bluetooth**: Turns off Bluetooth functionality for connecting devices like headphones, keyboards, and mice.

3. **Cellular Networks** (if applicable): Disables mobile data and cellular communication on devices with cellular connectivity, such as laptops with built-in LTE modems.

4. **Other Wireless Communications**: This may include GPS and near-field communication (NFC) on certain devices.

Enable/Disable Airplane Mode via Quick Settings

The Quick Settings menu offers the fastest way to toggle airplane mode.

1. **Open Quick Settings**:

   o Press **Windows + A** or click the **Network and Volume icon** in the taskbar.

2. **Toggle Airplane Mode**:

   o Click the **Airplane mode** button (it resembles an airplane icon). When enabled, the icon will highlight, and wireless connections will be disabled.

4

Software & Applications

How Do I Install a New Application on Windows 11?

How Do I Uninstall an Application in Windows 11?

How Do I Manage Startup Applications?

How Do I Set Default Apps for Specific File Types?

How Do I Update Installed Applications

How Do I Fix Compatibility Issues with Older Apps?

How Do I Use the Microsoft Store to Download Apps?

How Do I Manage Background Applications?

How Do I Set Application Permissions?

How Do I Manage App Notifications?

How Do I Reset an Application in Windows 11?

How Do I Create a Desktop Shortcut for an App?

How Do I Pin Apps to the Start Menu?

How Do I Pin Apps to the Taskbar?

How Do I Use the Snipping Tool to Take Screenshots?

How Do I Manage App Notifications on Lock Screen?

How Do I Use the Clipboard History Feature?

How Do I Change the Default App for PDF Files?

How Do I Enable Dark Mode for Specific Apps?

How do I use copilot?

How do I copy and move files in Windows 11?

How do I use drag and drop to move or copy files?

How do I copy or move multiple files at once?

How do I move or copy files between different drives?

How do I create folders in Windows 11?

Chapter 4: Software & Applications

How Do I Install a New Application on Windows 11?

1. **Using Microsoft Store:**

   o **Open Microsoft Store:** Click the **Start** button and select the **Microsoft Store** app.

   o **Search for the App:** Use the search bar at the top to find the desired application.

   o **Install:** Click on the app, then select **Get** or **Install**. Follow any on-screen instructions.

2. **Using an Installer File:**

   o **Download the Installer:** Obtain the installer from the official website of the software.

   o **Run the Installer:** Locate the downloaded .exe or .msi file in **File Explorer**, right-click it, and select **Run as administrator**.

   o **Follow Installation Prompts:** Proceed through the installation wizard by following the on-screen instructions.

   o **Complete Installation:** Once installed, you can find the application in the **Start** menu or on your desktop.

How Do I Uninstall an Application in Windows 11?

1. **Via Settings:**

   o **Open Settings:** Press **Win + I** to open **Settings**.

   o **Navigate to Apps:** Click on **Apps** in the sidebar.

   o **Apps & Features:** Select **Apps & features**.

   o **Find the App:** Scroll through the list or use the search bar to locate the application.

   o **Uninstall:** Click the three-dot menu next to the app and select **Uninstall**. Follow any additional prompts.

2. **Via Control Panel:**

   o **Open Control Panel:** Press **Win + R**, type control, then press **Enter**.

   o **Programs and Features:** Click on **Uninstall a program** under **Programs**.

    o **Select and Uninstall:** Choose the application you wish to remove, click **Uninstall**, and follow the instructions.

How Do I Manage Startup Applications?

1. Via the Settings App

    o Press **Win + I** simultaneously to open the settings app.

    o In the **Settings** window, click on **Apps** in the left sidebar.

    o Within the **Apps** section, select **Startup**. This will display a list of all applications that can be configured to run at system startup.

    o You'll see a list of applications with toggle switches next to each one.

    o **Enable Startup:** Click the toggle switch **On** to allow the application to launch at startup.

    o **Disable Startup:** Click the toggle switch **Off** to prevent the application from running automatically when Windows starts.

2. Via Task Manager

    o Press **Ctrl + Shift + Esc** to launch **Task Manager**.

    o If it's the first time, click **More details** at the bottom.

    o Click on the **Startup Apps** tab to view all applications

    o Select an application you want to manage.

    o Click **Enable** or **Disable** at the bottom-right corner based on your preference.

    o Open **Settings** (**Win + I**), go to **Apps** > **Startup**.

    o Toggle the switches next to each application to enable or disable them at startup.

How Do I Set Default Apps for Specific File Types?

1. Open Settings:

    o Press **Win + I** to open **Settings**.

    o Navigate to **Apps** > **Default apps**.

Chapter 4: Software & Applications

2. Choose an App:

- o Scroll through the list or use the search bar to select the application you want to set as default.

3. Set Defaults by File Type:

- o Click on the app, and you'll see a list of file types it can handle.

- o Click on the file extension (e.g., .jpg, .pdf) and select the desired default app from the pop-up list.

4. Set Defaults by Protocol (Optional):

- o Similar to file types, you can set defaults for specific protocols like HTTP, HTTPS, etc.

How Do I Update Installed Applications

1. Via Microsoft Store:

- o **Open Microsoft Store:** Click the **Start** button and select the **Microsoft Store** app.

- o **Navigate to Library:** Click on your profile icon and select **Library**.

- o **Check for Updates:** Click on **Get updates** to see and install available updates for your Microsoft Store apps.

2. Using the Application's Built-in Updater:

- o **Open the App:** Launch the application you want to update.

- o **Check for Updates:** Look for an **Update** option in the app's menu, often under **Help** or **Settings**.

- o **Follow Prompts:** If an update is available, follow the on-screen instructions to install it.

3. Windows Update (for System Apps):

- o **Open Settings:** Press **Win + I**.

- o **Navigate to Windows Update:** Click on **Windows Update** in the sidebar.

- o **Check for Updates:** Click **Check for updates** to see if there are any system-related application updates.

How Do I Fix Compatibility Issues with Older Apps?

1. **Use Compatibility Mode:**

   o **Right-Click the App:** Locate the application's executable file, right-click it, and select **Properties**.

   o **Navigate to Compatibility Tab:** Click on the **Compatibility** tab.

   o **Enable Compatibility Mode:** Check **Run this program in compatibility mode for:** and select the appropriate Windows version from the dropdown.

   o **Apply Changes:** Click **Apply** and then **OK**.

2. **Use Windows Compatibility Troubleshooter:**

   o **Right-Click the App:** Select **Troubleshoot compatibility**.

   o **Follow the Wizard:** Choose whether to let Windows select a recommended setting or specify a compatibility mode manually.

3. **Install Necessary Dependencies:**

   o **Check for Required Frameworks:** Some older applications may require specific versions of .NET Framework or Visual C++ Redistributables. Download and install these from Microsoft's official website.

4. **Virtual Machines or Emulators:**

   o **Set Up a VM:** Use software like **VirtualBox** or **VMware** to create a virtual machine running an older version of Windows.

   o **Install the App:** Run the application within the virtual environment where it's compatible.

How Do I Use the Microsoft Store to Download Apps?

1. **Open Microsoft Store:**

   o Click the **Start** button and select the **Microsoft Store** app.

2. **Sign In:**

   o Sign in with your Microsoft account to access your

115

purchased apps and sync settings.

3. **Browse or Search:**

   o   Use the search bar at the top to find a specific app or browse through categories like **Apps**, **Games**, **Entertainment**, etc.

4. **Select the App:**

   o   Click on the application you wish to download to view its details.

5. **Install:**

   o   Click the **Get** or **Install** button. For paid apps, click the price button and follow the prompts to purchase.

   o   The app will download and install automatically. You can monitor the progress in the **Downloads** section.

6. **Launch the App:**

   o   Once installed, you can open the app directly from the Microsoft Store or find it in the **Start** menu.

How Do I Manage Background Applications?

1. **Open Settings:**

   o   Press **Win + I** to open **Settings**.

   o   Navigate to **Privacy & security** > **Background apps**.

2. **View Background Apps:**

   o   You'll see a list of applications that can run in the background.

3. **Toggle Background Permissions:**

   o   For each app, use the toggle switch to allow or prevent it from running in the background.

4. **Manage Individual App Permissions:**

   o   Click on an app to access more specific permissions and settings related to background activity.

5. **Using Task Manager:**

   o   Press **Ctrl + Shift + Esc** to open **Task Manager**.

o Under the **Processes** tab, you can see which apps are currently running and using resources. Right-click and select **End task** to stop an application.

How Do I Set Application Permissions?

1. **Open Settings:**

   o Press **Win + I** to open **Settings**.

   o Go to **Privacy & security**.

2. **Select a Permission Category:**

   o Categories include **Camera**, **Microphone**, **Location**, **Contacts**, **Calendar**, **Call history**, **Email**, **Messaging**, **Radios**, **Notifications**, etc.

3. **Manage Permissions:**

   o Click on a category (e.g., **Camera**).

   o Toggle the switch to allow or deny access to apps for that particular permission.

   o For more granular control, scroll down to see a list of apps and individually toggle permissions for each.

4. **App-Specific Settings:**

   o Some applications have their own permission settings within the app itself. Open the app and navigate to its **Settings** or **Preferences** to adjust permissions as needed.

How Do I Manage App Notifications?

1. **Open Settings:**

   o Press **Win + I** to open **Settings**.

   o Navigate to **System > Notifications**.

2. **Toggle Notifications On or Off:**

   o Use the main switch to enable or disable all notifications.

3. **Customize Notifications:**

   o Scroll down to see a list of apps that can send notifications.

117

o   Toggle the switch next to each app to allow or block its notifications.

4. **Advanced Settings:**

o   **Notification Sound:** Choose whether to play a sound for notifications.

o   **Notification Banners:** Decide if banners appear on the screen.

o   **Hide Notifications from the Lock Screen:** Control visibility when the device is locked.

5. **Focus Assist:**

o   Under **Focus assist**, set rules to automatically limit notifications during specific times or activities, such as when duplicating your display or playing a game.

How Do I Reset an Application in Windows 11?

1. **Open Settings:**

o   Press **Win + I** to open **Settings**.

o   Navigate to **Apps** > **Apps & features**.

2. **Find the Application:**

o   Scroll through the list or use the search bar to locate the app you want to reset.

3. **Access Advanced Options:**

o   Click the three-dot menu next to the app and select **Advanced options**.

4. **Reset the App:**

o   Scroll down to the **Reset** section.

o   Click the **Reset** button. A warning will appear indicating that the app's data will be deleted.

o   Confirm by clicking **Reset** again.

5. **Completion:**

o   Once the reset is complete, the app will restart with default settings.

Chapter 4: Software & Applications

How Do I Create a Desktop Shortcut for an App?

1. **Navigate to the Application:**

   o Open **File Explorer** and go to the application's installation folder (usually stored in C:\Program Files\).

2. **Locate the Executable:**

   o Find the application's executable file (e.g., AppName. exe).

3. **Create the Shortcut:**

   o Right-click the executable file, select **Show more options** (if applicable), then choose **Send to** > **Desktop (create shortcut)**.

4. **Rename the Shortcut:**

   o Right-click the newly created shortcut on the desktop and select **Rename** to give it a more recognizable name.

How Do I Pin Apps to the Start Menu?

Pinning apps to the Start menu allows you to access your frequently used applications quickly.

1. **Open the Start Menu:**

   o Click on the **Start** button or press the **Win** key.

2. **Navigate to All Apps:**

   o Click on **All apps** at the top-right corner of the Start menu.

3. **Locate the App:**

   o Scroll through the alphabetical list to find the application you wish to pin.

4. **Pin the App:**

   o Right-click on the app.

   o Select **Pin to Start** from the context menu.

5. **Confirm the Pin:**

   o The application tile should now be visible in the **Pinned** section of the Start menu.

Chapter 4: Software & Applications

How Do I Pin Apps to the Taskbar?

Pinning apps to the taskbar provides quick access to your most-used applications directly from the bottom of your screen.

Method 1: From the Start Menu

1. **Open the Start Menu:**

   o   Click on the **Start** button or press the **Win** key.

2. **Find the App:**

   o   Browse through the list of apps or use the **Search** bar to locate the application you want to pin.

3. **Pin the App:**

   o   **Right-Click Method:**

      ▪   Right-click on the desired app.

      ▪   Select **Pin to taskbar** from the context menu.

   o   **Alternative Method:**

      ▪   Left-click and drag the app to the taskbar until you see a highlight, then release to pin.

4. **Verify the Pin:**

   o   The app's icon should now appear on the taskbar for easy access.

Method 2: From a Running Application

1. **Launch the Application:**

   o   Open the application you wish to pin by clicking its icon in the Start menu or searching for it.

2. **Pin While Running:**

   o   **Right-Click Method:**

      ▪   While the application is open, its icon appears on the taskbar.

      ▪   Right-click on the app's taskbar icon.

      ▪   Select **Pin to taskbar** from the context menu.

3. **Verify the Pin:**

120

o The app's icon will remain on the taskbar even after closing the application, allowing quick access in the future.

Additional Tips:

- **Unpinning Apps:**

   o To remove an app from the taskbar, right-click on its icon and select **Unpin from taskbar**.

- **Rearranging Taskbar Icons:**

   o Click and drag the app icons on the taskbar to rearrange them to your preferred order.

How Do I Use the Snipping Tool to Take Screenshots?

The **Snipping Tool** allows you to capture screenshots in various formats, enabling easy sharing and editing.

1. **Open Snipping Tool:**

   o Press **Win + Shift + S** to launch the Snipping Tool.

   o Alternatively, search for **Snipping Tool** in the Start menu and open it.

2. **Choose Snip Type:**

   o At the top of the screen, select the type of snip you want:

      ▪ **Rectangular Snip:** Click and drag to select a rectangular area.

      ▪ **Freeform Snip:** Draw a freeform shape around the area you want to capture.

      ▪ **Window Snip:** Select a specific window to capture.

      ▪ **Full-screen Snip:** Capture the entire screen.

3. **Capture the Screenshot:**

   o Select the desired snip type and capture the area or window accordingly.

4. **Edit and Save:**

   o After capturing, the screenshot opens in the Snipping

Tool window.

o Use the available tools to annotate, highlight, or crop the image.

o Click **Save** to store the screenshot in your desired location.

Additional Tips:

- **Use Keyboard Shortcuts:** Familiarize yourself with keyboard shortcuts for quicker access to the Snipping Tool.

- **Copy to Clipboard:** After capturing, the screenshot is automatically copied to the clipboard, allowing you to paste it directly into documents or messages.

- **Customize Snipping Tool Settings:** Explore settings within the Snipping Tool to adjust capture delays and other preferences.

How Do I Manage App Notifications on Lock Screen?

Managing notifications on the lock screen ensures that sensitive information isn't displayed when your device is locked.

1. **Open Settings:**

   o Press **Win + I** to open **Settings**.

   o Navigate to **System > Notifications**.

2. **Scroll to Lock Screen Notifications:**

   o Under the **Notifications** section, find **Notifications on the lock screen**.

3. **Manage Notifications:**

   o Toggle **Show notifications on the lock screen** to **On** or **Off** based on your preference.

4. **Customize App Notifications:**

   o Click on **Advanced settings** (if available) to manage which apps can show notifications on the lock screen.

   o Toggle individual apps to allow or block their notifications from appearing when the device is locked.

Additional Tips:

☐ **Sensitive Information:** Disable lock screen notifications for apps that display sensitive information to enhance privacy.

☐ **Stay Informed:** Allow essential apps (e.g., calendar, reminders) to show notifications on the lock screen for quick access.

☐ **Review Regularly:** Periodically review and adjust lock screen notification settings as your app usage changes.

How Do I Use the Clipboard History Feature?

Clipboard history allows you to access a list of items you've copied, making it easier to reuse content across applications.

1. **Enable Clipboard History:**

   o Press **Win + I** to open **Settings**.

   o Navigate to **System** > **Clipboard**.

   o Toggle **Clipboard history** to **On**.

2. **Copy Content:**

   o Use **Ctrl + C** to copy text, images, or other supported content from any application.

3. **Access Clipboard History:**

   o Press **Win + V** to open the Clipboard history window.

4. **Paste from History:**

   o In the Clipboard history window, click on the item you want to paste. It will be inserted into your current application.

5. **Pin Items:**

   o Hover over an item in the Clipboard history and click the **Pin** icon to keep it permanently available, even after restarting your computer.

6. **Clear Clipboard History:**

   o In the **Clipboard** settings, click **Clear** to remove all items from the clipboard history.

Additional Tips:

☐ **Sync Across Devices:** Enable **Sync across devices** in

Clipboard settings to access your clipboard history on all your Windows devices.

☐ **Security Considerations:** Be cautious about what you copy to the clipboard, especially sensitive information, as clipboard history can store this data.

☐ **Use Keyboard Shortcuts:** Familiarize yourself with clipboard shortcuts to streamline your workflow.

How Do I Change the Default App for PDF Files?

Changing the default application for PDF files allows you to open PDFs with your preferred reader.

1. **Open Settings:**

   o Press **Win + I** to open **Settings**.

   o Navigate to **Apps** > **Default apps**.

2. **Search for PDF File Type:**

   o In the **Set defaults for applications** search bar, type .pdf.

3. **Select the Default App:**

   o Click on the current default application (e.g., **Microsoft Edge**) next to the .pdf file type.

4. **Choose Your Preferred PDF Reader:**

   o From the list of available applications, select your preferred PDF reader (e.g., **Adobe Acrobat Reader**, **Foxit Reader**).

5. **Confirm the Change:**

   o After setting your preferred browser for all relevant file and link types, close the Settings app.

Additional Tips:

☐ **Install New PDF Readers:** If your preferred PDF reader isn't listed, ensure it's installed on your system.

☐ **Use a Single Browser:** To avoid confusion, ensure that all relevant file and link types are associated with your preferred browser.

⬜ **Revert to Original App:** If needed, you can revert to the original default application by following the same steps.

How Do I Enable Dark Mode for Specific Apps?

While Windows 11 allows you to set a global Dark Mode, some applications offer the option to enable Dark Mode independently. Here's how to manage Dark Mode settings both system-wide and for individual applications:

Method 1: Enable Dark Mode System-Wide

1. **Open Settings:**

   o Press **Win + I** to open **Settings**.

   o Navigate to **Personalization** > **Colors**.

2. **Choose Your Mode:**

   o Under **Choose your mode**, select **Dark** from the dropdown menu.

   o Alternatively, set **Choose your default Windows mode** and **Choose your default app mode** both to **Dark** to apply Dark Mode system-wide and to all compatible applications.

Method 2: Enable Dark Mode for Specific Applications

1. **Open the Application:**

   o Launch the application you want to customize (e.g., Microsoft Office apps, Adobe applications).

2. **Access Application Settings:**

   o Navigate to the application's **Settings** or **Preferences** menu. This is usually found under **File** > **Options** or by clicking on a gear icon.

3. **Enable Dark Mode:**

   o Look for a **Theme** or **Appearance** section.

   o Select **Dark Mode** or a similar option to enable it specifically for that application. For *Example for Microsoft Word:*

   o Open **Word**.

o   Click on **File** > **Options**.

o   Under the **General** tab, find **Personalize your copy of Microsoft Office**.

o   Set **Office Theme** to **Dark Gray** or **Black**.

4. **Apply Changes:**

o   Save the settings and restart the application if necessary to apply Dark Mode.

Additional Tips:

☐ **Consistency Across Apps:** For a consistent Dark Mode experience, enable Dark Mode both system-wide and within individual applications that support it.

☐ **Update Applications:** Ensure that your applications are updated to the latest version to access Dark Mode features.

☐ **Use High Contrast Themes:** If Dark Mode is not available, consider using high contrast themes for better visibility and reduced eye strain.

How do I use copilot?

Microsoft Copilot in Windows 11 is an AI-powered assistant integrated into the operating system, designed to streamline tasks, improve productivity, and enhance your overall experience.

1. Accessing Windows Copilot

Once your system is updated, you can access Copilot directly from the taskbar.

• **Locate the Copilot Icon:**

o   Look for the **Copilot** icon on the taskbar.

o   If you don't see it, you might need to enable it:

• **Right-click** on an empty space in the taskbar.

• Select **Taskbar settings**.

• In the settings window, find **Copilot** and toggle it **On**.

• **Using Keyboard Shortcut:**

o   You can also open Copilot using a keyboard shortcut if available (e.g., Windows key + C). Check the latest documentation or settings for specific shortcuts.

2. Getting Started with Copilot

o   **Text Input:** Type your queries or commands into the Copilot text box.

o   **Voice Commands:** If enabled, you can speak your commands for hands-free interaction.

3. Common Queries

o   Set a reminder to review the monthly report every first Monday

o   Copilot, draft an email to our suppliers about the delayed shipment

How do I copy and move files in Windows 11?

Windows 11 provides several straightforward methods to copy and move files:

- **Drag and Drop:** Click and hold the file, drag it to the desired location, and release.

- **Copy and Paste:** Right-click the file, select "Copy" or "Cut," navigate to the destination folder, right-click, and choose "Paste."

- **Keyboard Shortcuts:** Use Ctrl + C to copy, Ctrl + X to cut, and Ctrl + V to paste files.

- **Ribbon Toolbar:** In File Explorer, use the "Home" tab to access copy, cut, and paste options.

How do I use drag and drop to move or copy files?

- **To Copy a File:**

    1. Open **File Explorer** and navigate to the file you want to copy.

    2. Click and hold the file with your mouse.

    3. Press and hold the Ctrl key (a plus sign "+" will appear next to the cursor).

4. Drag the file to the desired folder and release the mouse button.

5. Release the Ctrl key.

- **To Move a File:**

    1. Open **File Explorer** and navigate to the file you want to move.

    2. Click and hold the file with your mouse.

    3. Drag the file to the desired folder without holding the Ctrl key.

    4. Release the mouse button to move the file.

How do I copy or move multiple files at once?

1. Open **File Explorer** and navigate to the files you want to manage.

2. Select multiple files by:

    o Hold down the Ctrl key then click each file individually.

    o Hold down the Shift key then click the first and last files in a sequence to select all in between.

3. Use any of the methods mentioned above (drag and drop, copy and paste, etc.) to copy or move the selected files to the desired location.

How do I move or copy files between different drives?

- **Using Drag & Drop:**

    1. Connect the external drive or device to your computer.

    2. Open **File Explorer** and navigate to the files you want to move or copy.

    3. Select the files.

    4. Use Ctrl + C to copy or Ctrl + X to cut.

    5. Navigate to the external drive or device in File Explorer.

    6. Press Ctrl + V to paste the files.

- **Using Drag and Drop:**

128

1. Open **File Explorer** and arrange the windows so that both the source and destination drives/devices are visible.

2. Select the files you want to move or copy.

3. Drag the selected files to the destination drive or device.

   - **To Copy:** Hold the Ctrl key while dragging.

   - **To Move:** Simply drag without holding any keys.

How do I create folders in Windows 11?

Creating folders in Windows 11 is a fundamental task that helps you organize your files efficiently.

Using File Explorer

1. **Open File Explorer:**

   o Click on the **File Explorer** icon in the taskbar.

   o Alternatively, press **Win + E** on your keyboard.

2. **Navigate to Desired Location:**

   o Browse to the directory where you want to create the new folder (e.g., Documents, Desktop).

3. **Right-Click to Open Context Menu:**

   o Right-click on an empty space within the folder.

4. **Select "New" > "Folder":**

   o From the context menu, click **New** and then click on **Folder**.

5. **Name Your Folder:**

   o A new folder will appear with the name highlighted. Type your desired name and press **Enter**.

Using the Command Prompt

1. **Open Command Prompt:**

   o Press **Win + R**, type **cmd**, then press **Enter**.

2. **Navigate to Desired Directory:**

o   Use the **cd** command to change directories. For example:

```
cd c:\users\%username%\documents
```

3. Create the Folder:

o   Type the following command then press **Enter**:

mkdir **FolderName**

o   Replace **FolderName** with your desired folder name. **Example:**

```
mkdir ProjectFiles
```

How do I set up OneDrive?

OneDrive is Microsoft's cloud storage service that allows you to store files securely online, access them from any device, and share them with others. Integrated into Windows 11, OneDrive offers features such as automatic file synchronization, collaboration tools, and robust security measures to ensure your data is always accessible and protected.

Install & Setup:

1. Launch OneDrive and Sign In:

o   Click on the **OneDrive** icon in the system tray (bottom-right corner). If it's not visible, you can find it by clicking the up arrow to show hidden icons.

o   Click **Sign In,** Enter your Microsoft account email address and password.

2. Choose Folder Location:

o   By default, OneDrive creates a folder in your user directory (C:\ Users\YourName\ OneDrive). You can change this location.

3. **Select Folders to Sync:**

   o   Choose which folders you want to sync to your PC. You can select all or specific folders based on your preference.

4. **Complete Setup:**

   o   Finish the setup process. OneDrive will start syncing your selected folders automatically.

How do I Syncing Files and Folders in OneDrive?

Syncing files and folders with OneDrive allows you to access your documents, photos, and other data across all your devices.

Adding Files to OneDrive:

1. **Using File Explorer:**

   o   Open **File Explorer** and navigate to the **OneDrive** folder.

   o   Drag and drop files or folders into the OneDrive directory to start syncing them to the cloud.

2. **Saving Directly to OneDrive:**

   o   When saving a file from an application (e.g., Word, Excel), choose **OneDrive** as the save location.

How do I enable/disable Files On-Demand in OneDrive?

Files On-Demand is a feature in OneDrive that allows you to access all your files stored in the cloud without having to download them to your local device. This saves disk space on your computer and is useful when using a phone, tablet or mobile device with limited locak disk storage.

Enable Files On-Demand:

   o   **To Enable,** click the **OneDrive** icon in the system tray, then click the settings icon. Select **Settings** from the menu.

   o   In **Sync & Backup** tab, go down to **Advanced Settings**.

   o   Under **Files On-Demand,** click **Free up disk space**.

Chapter 4: Software & Applications

Disable Files On-Demand

- o **To Disable,** click the **OneDrive** icon in the system tray, then click the settings icon. Select **Settings** from the menu.

- o In **Sync & Backup** tab, go down to A**dvanced Settings**.

- o Under **Files On-Demand,** click **Download all files**.

- **Sync Status Indicators:**

Green Checkmark means file is available locally.

Cloud Icon means file is online-only.

Blue Circular Arrows means file is currently syncing.

How do I Access Files on OneDrive?

OneDrive allows you to organize your documents, photos, and other data efficiently across multiple devices and is integrated into File Explorer, providing a centralized location to view, edit, and organize your synced files. Additionally, you can access your OneDrive files through the web browser or the mobile app.

Via File Explorer:

- **Navigate to OneDrive:**

- o Open **File Explorer** and select **OneDrive** from the left-hand pane.

- **Organize Files:**

- o Create, move, copy, or delete files and folders just like any other directory on your PC.

Via OneDrive Web Interface:

- **Access Online:**

- o Visit onedrive.com

o   Sign in with your Microsoft Account

☐ **Manage Files:**

o   Upload, download, share, and organize your files directly from the browser.

Using the OneDrive Mobile App:

☐ **Download App:**

o   Available for iOS and Android.

☐ **Sync Across Devices:**

o   Access and manage your files on the go, ensuring consistency across all your devices.

How do I Share Files and Folders with OneDrive?

Sharing files and folders with OneDrive allows you to collaborate and distribute your documents, images, and other data efficiently with other users. Using OneDrive's sharing features, you can grant access to specific individuals or groups, set permissions for viewing or editing, and manage shared content directly from File Explorer, the OneDrive web interface, or the mobile app.

Sharing via File Explorer:

1. **Right-Click Method:**

o   Right-click the file or folder you want to share within the **OneDrive** folder.

o   Select **Share**.

2. **Choose Sharing Options:**

o   **Send Link:** Generate a shareable link.

o   **Permissions:** Decide if recipients can edit or only view the files.

o   **Expiration and Password:** (If available) Set link expiration dates and passwords for added security.

b. Sharing via OneDrive Web Interface:

1. **Select File/Folder:**

o   Click on the file or folder you wish to share.

2. **Click Share:**

   o Choose **Share** and follow similar steps as above to configure sharing options.

Managing Shared Files:

☐ **View Shared Files:**

   o In **File Explorer**, go to **OneDrive** > **Shared** to see files shared with you and by you.

☐ **Manage Access:**

   o Adjust permissions or stop sharing by right-clicking the shared item and selecting **Manage access**.

How do I Backup and Restore with OneDrive?

Backing up and restoring files using OneDrive safeguards your important documents, photos, and other data. By configuring OneDrive to automatically sync specific folders, you can ensure that your files are continuously backed up to the cloud, reducing the risk of data loss due to hardware failures or accidental deletions. Additionally, OneDrive offers tools to restore previous versions of files and recover deleted items, allowing you to retrieve data as needed.

Setting Up Folder Backup:

1. **Open OneDrive Settings:**

   o Click the **OneDrive** icon in the system tray, then click the settings icon. Select **Settings** from the menu.

2. **Go to Sync & Backup Tab:**

   o Click on **Manage backup**.

3. **Select Folders to Backup:**

   o Choose **Desktop**, **Documents**, and **Pictures** to automatically back them up to OneDrive.

Restoring Files:

☐ **From OneDrive Web:**

   o Navigate to onedrive.com

   o Locate the file, and download it.

☐ **From File Explorer:**

    o   Files synced to your PC are available directly in the **OneDrive** folder.

Managing OneDrive Storage

Checking Storage Usage:

1. **Via File Explorer:**

    o   Right-click the **OneDrive** folder and select **Properties** to see used and available space.

2. **Via OneDrive Settings:**

    o   Open **Settings** from the OneDrive system tray icon.

    o   Under the **Account** tab, view storage details.

3. **Via OneDrive Web:**

    o   Navigate to onedrive.com

    o   Click on **Settings** (gear icon), and select **Options** to view storage usage.

Upgrading Storage:

☐ **Free Storage:** Typically offers 5 GB for free.

☐ **Paid Plans:** Upgrade to Microsoft 365 for additional storage (e.g., 1 TB per user).

Managing Storage:

☐ **Remove Unnecessary Files:**

    o   Delete files you no longer need to free up space.

☐ **Use Files On-Demand:**

    o   Store files online-only to save local disk space.

How do I use OneDrive with Microsoft Office?

Using OneDrive with Microsoft Office allows you to save, access, and collaborate on your documents across different devices with other users. Integration between OneDrive and Office applications such as Word, Excel, and PowerPoint enables automatic saving of your work to the cloud, ensuring that your latest changes are available wherever you go.

Additionally, this integration supports real-time collaboration, allowing multiple users to work on the same document simultaneously.

Saving Directly to OneDrive:

☐ **From Office Applications:**

- o When saving a document, select **OneDrive** as the destination to ensure it's backed up and accessible across devices.

Real-Time Collaboration:

☐ **Collaborate with Others:**

- o Multiple users can edit Office documents simultaneously when stored in OneDrive, enhancing teamwork and productivity.

How do I Set up Personal Vault in OneDrive?

OneDrive's Personal Vault is a secure, protected space within your OneDrive that provides extra security for your sensitive files, such as financial documents, IDs, or personal photos.

You can access it using a variety of ways.

On Windows:

1. Open **File Explorer**.

2. Locate **OneDrive** in the navigation pane and click it.

3. Double click on **Personal Vault**.

4. When opening Personal Vault for the first time, follow the on-screen instructions to set it up:

- o Enter your Microsoft account credentials.

- o Complete **two-step verification** (via text, email, or authenticator app).

5. Personal Vault is now ready for use.

On Mobile (iOS/Android):

1. Open the **OneDrive app**.

2. Tap **Files** and locate **Personal Vault**.

3. Follow the prompts to set up the Vault:

    ○   Verify your identity using two-step authentication (e.g., SMS code or biometric login).

4. Once set up, the Vault will appear as a folder within your OneDrive.

On Web:

1. Open your web browser, go to `onedrive.com` and sign in.

2. In the **Files** section, locate and click on **Personal Vault**.

3. Follow the on-screen instructions to enable the Vault:

    ○   Verify your identity using a security code sent to your email or phone.

4. Personal Vault will now be accessible in your OneDrive online.

How do I Add Files to Personal Vault in OneDrive?

Adding files to Personal Vault in OneDrive is a simple yet effective way to secure sensitive documents, photos, or any important data with an additional layer of protection.

Let's take a look at how to add files to the vault.

On Windows:

1. Drag and drop files into the **Personal Vault** folder in File Explorer.

On Mobile:

1. Open the OneDrive app and tap **Files**.

2. Tap the **+ (Add)** button, then select:

    ○   **Upload**: To upload files to Personal Vault.

    ○   **Scan**: To directly scan a document (e.g., ID) and save it to the Vault.

3. Choose **Personal Vault** as the save location.

On Web:

1. Navigate to the Personal Vault folder.

2. Click **Add New**, then select **Upload**. Select the files you want to upload.

Chapter 4: Software & Applications

How do I Access Files in Personal Vault in OneDrive?

Accessing files in Personal Vault on OneDrive is a secure process designed to protect your most sensitive documents while keeping them easily available whenever needed.

On Windows:

1. Open File Explorer and click **Personal Vault** under OneDrive.

2. Enter your verification method to unlock. (PIN, biometric, or SMS/email code).

3. Access your files as needed.

On Mobile:

1. Open the OneDrive app and tap **Personal Vault**.

2. Use your chosen authentication method (PIN, biometric, etc.) to unlock the Vault.

3. Open, share, or move files as needed.

On Web:

1. Click on **Personal Vault** in the Files section of OneDrive.

2. Complete the two-step verification.

3. Access your files securely.

How do I Secure and Lock Personal Vault in OneDrive?

Securing and locking Personal Vault in OneDrive is essential to ensure the privacy and safety of your sensitive files. Personal Vault is a protected folder within OneDrive that uses advanced encryption and requires additional identity verification, such as a PIN, biometric login, or a one-time code, to access its contents.

- **Auto-Lock**: After a period of inactivity (default: 20 minutes), Personal Vault will lock automatically.

- **Manual Lock**:

   o On Windows: Right-click the Vault and select **Lock Personal Vault**.

   o On Mobile: Tap the lock icon within the Personal Vault.

   o On Web: Close the Vault or click the lock icon.

How do I compress and extract files?

Compressing and extracting files in Windows 11 allows you to reduce the size of files and folders for easier storage and sharing, as well as to access the contents of compressed files. Windows 11 includes built-in tools for compressing (zipping) and extracting (unzipping) files, making the process straightforward without the need for additional software.

Compressing Files and Folders

Compressing files and folders reduces their size, making them easier to store and share.

1. **Open File Explorer:**

   o   Press **Win + E** or click the **File Explorer** icon on the taskbar.

2. **Navigate to the Files/Folders:**

   o   Browse to the location of the files or folders you want to compress.

3. **Select Files/Folders:**

   o   Click to select a single file or folder.

   o   To select multiple items, hold down the **Ctrl** key and click each item you want to include.

4. **Right-Click Selection:**

   o   Right-click on one of the selected files or folders to open the context menu.

5. **Choose "Compress to":**

   o   From the slideout menu, select **Zip File**.

6. **Name the ZIP File:**

   o   A new ZIP file will appear in the same location with the name highlighted.

   o   Type a desired name for your ZIP file and press **Enter**.

Extracting (Unzipping) Files and Folders

Extracting files from a ZIP archive restores them to their original size and structure.

Chapter 4: Software & Applications

1. **Locate the Archive file:**

   o Open **File Explorer** and navigate to the ZIP file you wish to extract.

   o Windows will extract: ZIP (.zip), CAB (.cab), RAR (.rar), 7Z (.7z), TAR (.tar), GZ (.gz), TAR.GZ (.tar.gz), ISO (.iso), LZH (.lzh), ARJ (.arj).

2. **Right-Click the ZIP File:**

   o Right-click on the ZIP file to open the context menu.

3. **Choose "Extract All":**

   o Click on **Extract All** from the context menu.

4. **Select Extraction Location:**

   o In the **Extract Compressed (Zipped) Folders** dialog box, choose the destination where you want the files to be extracted.

   o You can click **Browse** to select a different folder.

5. **Start Extraction:**

   o Click **Extract** to begin the process.

6. **Access Extracted Files:**

   o Once extraction is complete, the extracted files will open in a new File Explorer window.

5 Installation & Upgrade

How do I install Windows 11 on my PC?

How do I Activate Windows 11?

How do I upgrade from Windows 10 to Windows 11?

How do I create a bootable USB for Windows 11?

How do I reset Windows 11?

How Do I Enter Windows Recovery Environment (WinRE)?

Chapter 5: Installation & Upgrade

How do I install Windows 11 on my PC?

Installing Windows 11 involves several key steps to ensure a smooth and successful installation. Here's how you can do it:

Step 1: Verify System Requirements

- **Check Compatibility:** Ensure your PC meets the minimum system requirements for Windows 11:

    o **Processor:** Compatible 64-bit processor
    o **RAM:** 4GB
    o **Storage:** 64GB
    o **TPM:** Version 2.0
    o **Secure Boot:** Supported

- **Use Microsoft's PC Health Check Tool:** Download and run the tool to confirm compatibility.

    aka.ms/GetPCHealthCheckApp

Step 2: Backup Important Data

- **Protect Your Files:** Use an external hard drive, USB flash drive, or a cloud storage service to back up essential files to prevent data loss during installation.

Step 3: Download the Windows 11 Installation Assistant

- **Go to the Download Page:**

    www.microsoft.com/software-download/windows11

- **Download the Tool:** Click on the **"Download Now"** button under the **Installation Assistant** section.

Step 4: Run the Installation Assistant

- **Launch the Tool:** Locate the downloaded Windows11InstallationAssistant.exe file in your Downloads folder and double-click to open it.

- **Accept Terms:** Read and accept the license terms when prompted.

Step 5: Begin Installation

- **Check for Updates:** The Installation Assistant will verify updates and compatibility.

- **Start Installation:** Click **"Accept and Install"** to proceed. The necessary Windows 11 files will download, which may take some time based on your internet speed.

Step 6: Follow On-Screen Prompts

- **Installation Options:** Choose whether to keep your personal files and apps or perform a clean installation.

- **Proceed with Installation:** Click **"Install"** to begin. Your PC will restart multiple times during the process.

Step 7: Complete Setup

- **Initial Configuration:** After installation, follow the on-screen instructions to set up Windows 11, including configuring your region, keyboard layout, and signing in with your Microsoft account.

Step 8: Activate Windows 11

- **Navigate to Activation:** Go to **Settings > System > Activation**.

- **Ensure Activation:** Verify that Windows 11 is activated. If not, click **"Change product key"** and enter your 25-character product key.

How do I Activate Windows 11?

Step 1: Open the Settings App

1. **Press Win + I**

Step 2: Navigate to Activation Settings

1. **Select "System":**

   o In the **Settings** window, click on **"System"** in the left-hand sidebar.

2. **Choose "Activation":**

   o Scroll down within the **System** settings and click on **"Activation."**

Step 3: Check Activation Status

- **If Windows is Already Activated:**

   o If you see **"Windows is activated with a digital license"** or **"Windows is activated with a digital license linked to your Microsoft account."** No further action is needed.

☐ **If Windows is Not Activated:**

  o You will see options to **"Activate"** or **"Change product key."**

Step 4: Activate Windows

Using a Digital License

1. **Sign In to Microsoft Account (If Prompted):**

  o If your digital license is linked to your Microsoft account, ensure you are signed in.

2. **Automatic Activation:**

  o Windows should automatically detect the digital license and activate itself.

  o **No further steps are required** if the activation is successful.

Using a Product Key

1. **Click on "Change product key":**

  o This option allows you to enter a 25-character product key.

2. **Enter Your Product Key:**

  o Input your **25-character Windows 11 product key** (e.g., XXXXX-XXXXX-XXXXX-XXXXX-XXXXX).

3. **Click "Next":**

  o After entering the product key, click **"Next"** to proceed.

4. **Accept License Terms:**

  o Read and accept the license terms when prompted.

5. **Activate:**

  o Click **"Activate"** to begin the activation process.

  o **Ensure your PC is connected to the internet** during this process.

6. **Confirmation:**

  o Once activated, you will see a confirmation message

indicating that **"Windows is activated."**

Using the Command Prompt for Activation (Advanced)

- Open **Command Prompt** as an administrator.

- **Install Product Key:**

  - o Enter the command:

    ```
    slmgr.vbs /ipk YOUR-PRODUCT-KEY
    ```

- **Activate Windows:**

  - o Enter the command:

    ```
    slmgr.vbs /ato
    ```

Replace YOUR-PRODUCT-KEY with your actual 25-character product key.

Activate Windows 11 in a Volume Licensing Environment (For Businesses and Organizations)

Businesses and organizations using Volume Licensing can activate Windows 11 through a Key Management Service (KMS) or Multiple Activation Key (MAK).

A. KMS Activation

KMS is a local activation service that allows organizations to activate systems within their network without connecting to Microsoft's activation servers over the internet.

1. **Set Up a KMS Host:**

   - o Install the KMS host key on a server within your network.

   - o Activate the KMS host with Microsoft.

2. **Configure Client PCs:**

   - o Ensure client PCs are configured to locate the KMS host.

   - o Use the following command in Command Prompt (run as administrator):

     ```
     slmgr.vbs /skms your-kms-server-address
     ```

3. **Activate Clients:**

   - o Windows will automatically attempt to activate with the

KMS host during the next periodic check-in.

B. MAK Activation

MAK is a one-time activation method where systems activate directly with Microsoft's activation servers over the internet or by phone.

1. **Obtain a MAK Key:**

    o   Acquire a Multiple Activation Key from your Volume Licensing Service Center.

2. **Enter the MAK Key:**

    o   Open **Command Prompt** as an administrator.

    o   Enter the following command:

    ```
    slmgr.vbs /ipk YOUR-MAK-KEY
    ```

3. **Activate Windows:**

    o   After installing the MAK key, activate Windows by running:

    ```
    slmgr.vbs /ato
    ```

4. **Confirmation:**

    o   A message will confirm successful activation.

Note: Volume Licensing methods are intended for organizations and may require coordination with your IT department or Microsoft representative.

How do I upgrade from Windows 10 to Windows 11?

Before beginning the upgrade process, it's essential to check your device's compatibility and ensure you meet the system requirements. The key requirements are:

*   **Processor:** A compatible 64-bit processor with at least 1 GHz clock speed and 2 or more cores. Supported processors include Intel 8th Gen and newer, AMD Ryzen 2000 series and newer, and select Qualcomm Snapdragon chips.

*   **Memory (RAM):** A minimum of 4 GB.

*   **Storage:** At least 64 GB of available storage.

*   **System Firmware:** UEFI firmware with Secure Boot capability.

*   **Trusted Platform Module (TPM):** TPM version 2.0 is required.

Microsoft has reiterated that this requirement is non-negotiable, citing security benefits.

- **Graphics Card:** DirectX 12 compatible graphics with a WDDM 2.0 driver.

- **Display:** A high-definition (720p) display that is greater than 9 inches diagonally, with 8 bits per color channel.

Follow these steps to ensure a smooth upgrade:

Step 1: Check Compatibility

- **PC Health Check Tool:** Download and run the PC Health Check tool to verify if your Windows 10 PC meets the requirements for Windows 11.

  `aka.ms/GetPCHealthCheckApp`

Step 2: Backup Your Data

- **Secure Your Files:** Back up important data to an external drive or cloud storage to prevent potential data loss during the upgrade.

Step 3: Update Windows 10

- **Open Settings:** Press Win + I to open the Settings app.

- **Navigate to Updates:** Go to **Update & Security > Windows Update**.

- **Check for Updates:** Click **"Check for updates"** and install any pending updates to ensure your system is up to date.

Step 4: Access Windows Update

- **Stay in Settings:** Remain in **Update & Security > Windows Update** after updating Windows 10.

Step 5: Check for Windows 11 Update

- **Find the Update:** Click **"Check for updates."** If Windows 11 is available for your device, it will appear as an optional update.

Step 6: Download and Install

- **Start Upgrade:** Click **"Download and install"** under the Windows 11 update.

- **Follow Prompts:** Follow the on-screen instructions to begin the upgrade process. This may involve several restarts.

Step 7: Complete Installation

- **Final Setup:** After installation completes, go through the setup process to configure your preferences and settings.

Step 8: Verify Activation

- **Check Activation Status:** Navigate to **Settings > System > Activation** to ensure Windows 11 is activated. If not, enter your product key.

Step 9: Rollback Upgrade (If Necessary)

- **Revert to Windows 10:** If you encounter significant issues after upgrading, you can rollback to Windows 10 within 10 days:

  o   Go to **Settings > System > Recovery**.

  o   Select **"Go back"** to return to Windows 10.

How do I create a bootable USB for Windows 11?

Creating a bootable USB drive for Windows 11 allows you to install the operating system on compatible devices. Here's how to create one:

Step 1: Download the Media Creation Tool

- **Visit the Download Page:** Go to the Microsoft Windows 11 download page.

  www.microsoft.com/software-download/windows11

- **Download the Tool:** Scroll to the **"Create Windows 11 Installation Media"** section and click **"Download now."**

Step 2: Run the Media Creation Tool

- **Launch the Tool:** Locate the downloaded **MediaCreationToolW11.exe** file and double-click to open it.

- **Accept Terms:** Read and accept the license terms when prompted.

Step 3: Choose Installation Media

- **Select Option:** Choose **"Create installation media (USB flash drive, DVD, or ISO file) for another PC"** and click **"Next."**

Step 4: Select Language, Edition, and Architecture

- **Customize Settings:** Choose your preferred language, Windows 11 edition, and architecture (64-bit).

- **Proceed:** Click **"Next."**

Step 5: Choose Media Type

- **Select USB Flash Drive:** Choose **"USB flash drive"** as the media type and click **"Next."**

Step 6: Select USB Drive

- **Insert USB Drive:** Plug in a USB flash drive with at least 8GB of storage.

- **Choose Drive:** Select the USB drive from the list and click **"Next."**

Step 7: Create Bootable USB

- **Download and Create:** The tool will download Windows 11 and create the bootable USB drive. This process may take some time depending on your internet speed.

Step 8: Complete the Process

- **Finish Up:** Once the creation is complete, click **"Finish."**

- **Safely Eject:** Safely eject the USB drive from your PC. It is now ready for use.

Step 9: Use the Bootable USB

- **Install Windows 11:** Insert the bootable USB into the target PC, restart the computer, and boot from the USB to begin the Windows 11 installation process.

How do I reset Windows 11?

Before proceeding with resetting Windows 11 to factory settings, it's essential to backup data to prevent data loss and ensure a smooth process.

Method 1: Reset via Settings

This is the most straightforward and commonly used method to reset Windows 11.

Step 1: Open Settings

1. **Press Win + I:**

   o This keyboard shortcut opens the **Settings** app directly.

Step 2: Navigate to Recovery Options

1. **Go to System Settings:**

   o In the **Settings** window, click on **"System"** in the left sidebar.

2. **Access Recovery:**

   o Scroll down and select **"Recovery."**

Step 3: Start the Reset Process

1. **Find Reset This PC:**

   o Under the **Recovery options**, locate **"Reset this PC."**

2. **Click on Reset:**

   o Click the **"Reset PC"** button to initiate the process.

Step 4: Choose Reset Options

1. **Choose an Option:**

   o **Keep my files:**

      ▪ Removes apps and settings but keeps your personal files. Choose this option if you want to fix system issues without losing personal files like documents or pictures. It removes installed apps and resets settings to default but keeps your user data intact. Ideal for resolving software problems while preserving your data.

   o **Remove everything:**

      ▪ Removes all personal files, apps, and settings. Select this for a complete reset that returns the PC to its factory condition. This is best when preparing to sell the device, addressing severe malware issues, or starting fresh. Use with caution.

2. **Select Cloud or Local Reinstall:**

o **Cloud download:**

  ▪ Downloads the latest version of Windows 11 from Microsoft servers. Requires internet connection and more data.

o **Local reinstall:**

  ▪ Reinstalls Windows 11 from the local system files. Faster and doesn't require internet.

Step 5: Follow On-Screen Instructions

1. Additional Settings:

  o Depending on your choices, you may see additional settings like deleting files from all drives or cleaning the drives.

2. Confirm Reset:

  o Review your selections and click **"Next"** or **"Reset"** to begin the process.

3. Wait for Completion:

  o The reset process will take some time. Your PC will restart multiple times during this period.

4. Setup Windows:

  o After the reset, follow the on-screen instructions to set up Windows 11.

Method 2: Reset Using Installation Media

This method is useful if your PC cannot boot into Windows or if you prefer a clean installation.

Step 1: Create Windows 11 Installation Media

1. Download the Media Creation Tool:

  o Visit the Microsoft Windows 11 Download Page.

  o Scroll to **"Create Windows 11 Installation Media"** and click **"Download now."**

2. Run the Tool:

  o Locate the downloaded MediaCreationToolW11. exe and double-click to run.

3. Create Bootable USB/DVD:

o Follow the prompts to create a bootable USB flash drive (minimum 8GB) or DVD.

Step 2: Boot from Installation Media

1. Insert Installation Media:

o Plug in the bootable USB drive or insert the DVD into your PC.

2. Restart Your PC:

o Restart your computer.

3. Access Boot Menu:

o Press the appropriate key (commonly F12, F2, Del, or Esc) during startup to access the boot menu.

4. Select Boot Device:

o Choose the USB drive or DVD as the boot device.

Step 3: Initiate Reset Process

1. Windows Setup Screen:

o Once booted, you'll see the Windows Setup screen.

2. Choose Language and Keyboard:

o Select your preferred language, time, and keyboard settings. Click **"Next."**

3. Install Now:

o Click the **"Install now"** button.

4. Activation:

o Enter your Windows 11 product key when prompted or choose **"I don't have a product key"** if reusing a digital license.

5. Select Installation Type:

o Choose **"Custom: Install Windows only (advanced)"** for a clean installation.

6. Delete Partitions:

- o Delete existing partitions if you want to remove all data and perform a full factory reset. **Caution:** This will erase all data on the selected partitions.

7. Select Installation Drive:

- o Choose the drive where Windows 11 will be installed and click **"Next."**

8. Complete Installation:

- o Follow the on-screen instructions to complete the installation. Your PC will restart several times.

How Do I Enter Windows Recovery Environment (WinRE)?

The Windows Recovery Environment (WinRE) is a lightweight operating system used for troubleshooting and repairing problems in Windows. It includes tools for startup repair, resetting the PC, accessing a command prompt, restoring a system image, and managing advanced boot options.

There are various methods to access WinRE depending on what the problem is.

Method 1: From Settings

1. Open the **Settings** app (press Win + I).

2. Navigate to **System > Recovery**.

3. Under the **Advanced startup** section, click **Restart now**.

4. Select **Troubleshoot > Advanced options** when the recovery environment loads.

Method 2: From the Sign-In Screen

1. On the sign-in screen, click the **Power** button in the lower-right corner.

2. Hold down the **Shift key** and click **Restart**.

3. Your PC will restart and load into the recovery environment.

Method 3: Using Installation Media or a Recovery Drive

1. Insert a Windows 11 installation media or recovery drive (USB).

2. Restart your PC and boot from the installation media. (You may need to press a specific key, such as **F11, F12** or **Esc**, to access the boot menu. Refer to your manufacturer's instructions for actual key press).

3. On the setup screen, select **Repair your computer** to access WinRE.

Method 4: Automatic Recovery (When Windows Fails to Boot)

1. If Windows cannot boot properly after multiple attempts, it will automatically enter the recovery environment. This method is useful if Windows won't start.

    *   Turn on your PC and let it boot.

    *   As soon as you see the Windows logo or loading screen, hold down the power button until the screen goes blank.

    *   Repeat this process three times.

    *   On the third restart, Windows will detect the repeated boot failures and load the Recovery Environment automatically.

2. Once in WinRE, you can access troubleshooting and repair options.

6 Advanced Settings & Tools

How do I use Disk Management to manage my drives?

How do I access and use the Task Scheduler?

How do I manage Virtual Memory (Paging File)?

How do I adjust Adjusting Power Settings?

How do I use the Registry Editor safely?

How do I access and use the Group Policy Editor?

How do I Refresh Windows 11 Components?

How do I Calibrate my Monitor?

How do I enable Virtualization?

How do I Create Virtual Machines with Hyper-V

How do I Create Virtual Machines with VirtualBox?

Chapter 6: Advanced Settings & Tools

How do I use Disk Management to manage my drives?

Disk Management is a built-in Windows utility that allows you to manage disk partitions, volumes, and drive configurations.

Accessing Disk Management

- Press Win + X and select **Disk Management** from the Quick Access Menu.

- **Creating a New Partition (Volume):**

  o **Step 1:** In Disk Management, locate the unallocated space on your disk.

  o **Step 2:** Right-click on the unallocated space and select **New Simple Volume**.

  o **Step 3:** Follow the New Simple Volume Wizard to specify the volume size, assign a drive letter, and format the partition with your preferred file system (e.g., NTFS).

- **Deleting a Partition (Volume):**

  o **Step 1:** Right-click on the partition you wish to delete.

  o **Step 2:** Select **Delete Volume**.

  o **Step 3:** Confirm the deletion. **Warning:** This action will erase all data on the partition. Ensure you have backed up important data before proceeding.

- **Formatting a Drive:**

  o **Step 1:** Right-click on the partition you want to format.

  o **Step 2:** Select **Format**.

  o **Step 3:** Choose the desired file system, allocation unit size, and provide a volume label.

  o **Step 4:** Decide whether to perform a quick format and click **OK** to proceed.

- **Changing Drive Letters and Paths:**

  o **Step 1:** Right-click on the partition whose drive letter you want to change.

  o **Step 2:** Select **Change Drive Letter and Paths**.

  o **Step 3:** Click **Change**, select a new drive letter from the dropdown menu, and confirm.

- **Extending or Shrinking Volumes:**

  - o **Extend Volume:**

    - □ **Step 1:** Right-click on the partition you wish to extend.

    - □ **Step 2:** Select **Extend Volume** and follow the wizard to add more unallocated space.

  - o **Shrink Volume:**

    - □ **Step 1:** Right-click on the partition you want to shrink.

    - □ **Step 2:** Select **Shrink Volume** and specify the amount to reduce.

- **Initializing a New Disk:**

  - o When a new physical disk is connected, Disk Management prompts you to initialize it.

  - o Choose between **MBR (Master Boot Record)** and **GPT (GUID Partition Table)** based on your system's requirements.

  - o **GPT** is recommended for disks larger than 2 TB and systems using UEFI.

- **Converting Disk Types:**

  - o **Convert to Dynamic Disk:**

    - □ **Step 1:** Right-click on the disk (e.g., Disk 1) you want to convert.

    - □ **Step 2:** Select **Convert to Dynamic Disk**.

    - □ **Step 3:** Follow the prompts to complete the conversion.

  - o **Convert to Basic Disk:**

    - □ **Step 1:** Right-click on the dynamic disk.

    - □ **Step 2:** Select **Convert to Basic Disk**. **Note:** This will erase all volumes on the disk.

Best Practices and Tips

- **Backup Data:** Always back up important data before making changes to disk partitions to prevent data loss.

- **Use GPT for Modern Systems:** For disks larger than 2 TB or systems with UEFI firmware, GPT is preferred over MBR.

- **Manage Disk Space Efficiently:** Regularly review and adjust partitions to optimize storage usage.

- **Avoid Interruptions:** Ensure your computer remains powered on during disk operations to prevent corruption.

How do I access and use the Task Scheduler?

Task Scheduler is a Windows utility that allows you to automate tasks by scheduling scripts, programs, or commands to run at specific times or in response to certain events.

Accessing Task Scheduler

- **Method 1:**

    o   Press Win + R to open the Run dialog.

    o   Type taskschd.msc and press **Enter**.

- **Method 2:**

    o   Click the **Start** button and search for **Task Scheduler**.

    o   Select **Task Scheduler** from the search results.

- **Method 3:**

    o   Press Win + X and select **Task Scheduler** from the Quick Access Menu.

Navigating the Task Scheduler Interface

- **Task Scheduler Library:** The main section where all scheduled tasks are organized. You can browse through folders to find specific tasks.

- **Actions Pane:** Located on the right, it provides options to create, import, and manage tasks.

- **Details Pane:** Displays detailed information about the selected task, including triggers, actions, conditions, and settings.

Creating a Basic Task

158

- **Step 1:** In the Task Scheduler window, click **Create Basic Task** in the Actions pane.

- **Step 2:** Enter a **Name** and an optional **Description** for the task. Click **Next**.

- **Step 3:** Choose a **Trigger** (e.g., Daily, Weekly, Monthly, One time, When the computer starts, When I log on, When a specific event is logged). Click **Next**.

- **Step 4:** Set the **Start date and time** and configure any additional scheduling options based on the chosen trigger. Click **Next**.

- **Step 5:** Select an **Action**:

  - **Start a program:** Launch a specific application or script.

- **Step 6:** Specify the **Program/script** to run and add any necessary **arguments** or **start-in** paths. Click **Next**.

- **Step 7:** Review the summary of the task and click **Finish** to create the task.

Creating an Advanced Task

For more complex tasks with multiple triggers, conditions, or actions:

- **Step 1:** In the Task Scheduler window, click **Create Task** instead of **Create Basic Task**.

- **Step 2:** In the **General** tab, provide a **Name** and **Description**. Choose the security options, such as running whether the user is logged on or not, and whether to run with highest privileges.

- **Step 3:** Navigate to the **Triggers** tab and click **New** to add multiple triggers as needed.

- **Step 4:** Go to the **Actions** tab and click **New** to define multiple actions for the task.

- **Step 5:** Configure settings in the **Conditions** and **Settings** tabs to specify conditions like idle time, power state, and task behavior upon failure or success.

- **Step 6:** Click **OK** to save the advanced task. You may be prompted to enter your user credentials.

Managing Existing Tasks

- **Viewing Tasks:** Browse through the Task Scheduler Library to find existing tasks. Expand folders to locate specific tasks.

- **Running a Task Manually:**

  o Right-click on the desired task and select **Run**.

- **Disabling or Enabling a Task:**

  o Right-click on the task and choose **Disable** or **Enable** as needed.

- **Editing a Task:**

  o Right-click the task and select **Properties** to modify triggers, actions, conditions, or settings.

- **Deleting a Task:**

  o Right-click the task and select **Delete** to remove it permanently.

Common Use Cases

- **Automated Backups:**

  o Schedule scripts or backup software to run at regular intervals, ensuring data is backed up without manual intervention.

- **System Maintenance:**

  o Automate disk cleanup, defragmentation, or system scans during off-peak hours to optimize performance.

- **Software Updates:**

  o Schedule the installation of updates or patches to maintain system security and functionality.

- **Launching Applications:**

  o Automatically start essential applications or services when the computer boots or a user logs in.

- **Notifications and Alerts:**

  o Trigger notifications or alerts based on specific system events or conditions.

Best Practices

- **Use Descriptive Names:** Clearly name your tasks to easily identify their purpose.

- **Test Tasks:** After creating a task, manually run it to ensure it functions as expected.

- **Monitor Task History:** Enable task history to track executions, successes, and failures for troubleshooting.

- **Limit Task Privileges:** Run tasks with the least privileges necessary to minimize security risks.

- **Organize Tasks:** Use folders within the Task Scheduler Library to categorize and manage tasks effectively.

How do I manage Virtual Memory (Paging File)?

Virtual memory allows the system to use disk space as additional RAM, which can help improve performance, especially when physical RAM is limited.

1. **In the Performance Options Dialog:**

   o   Go to the **Advanced** tab.

2. **Virtual Memory Section:**

   o   Click on the **Change** button under **Virtual memory**.

3. **Adjust Paging File Size:**

   o   Uncheck **Automatically manage paging file size for all drives**.

   o   Select the drive where Windows is installed.

   o   Choose **Custom size** and set the **Initial size (MB)** and **Maximum size (MB)** based on your system's RAM:

      ▪   **Initial size:** Typically 1.5 times the amount of RAM.

      ▪   **Maximum size:** Up to 3 times the amount of RAM.

   o   Click **Set** and then **OK** to apply the changes.

   o   **Note:** Restart your computer to apply the new settings.

How do I adjust Adjusting Power Settings?

Power settings can influence system performance, especially on laptops where power consumption is a concern.

1. **Open Power Options:**

   o Press Win + I to open Settings.

   o Navigate to **System** > **Power & battery**.

2. **Choose a Power Plan:**

   o **Balanced:** Automatically balances performance with energy consumption.

   o **Power saver:** Reduces performance to extend battery life.

   o **High performance:** Maximizes performance, consuming more energy.

3. **Creating a Custom Power Plan:**

   o Click on **Additional power settings**.

   o Select **Create a power plan** and configure settings to prioritize performance or energy savings as needed.

How do I use the Registry Editor safely?

The **Registry Editor** is a tool in Windows that allows you to view and modify the system registry—a hierarchical database that stores low-level settings for the operating system and installed applications. It's crucial you use the Registry Editor with caution.

Accessing the Registry Editor

1. **Open Registry Editor:**

   o Press Win + R to open the Run dialog.

   o Type regedit and press **Enter**.

   o If prompted by User Account Control (UAC), click **Yes** to allow.

Understanding the Registry Structure

The registry is divided into several **hives**, each containing keys and values:

   ☐ **HKEY_CLASSES_ROOT (HKCR):** Contains information about registered applications, file associations, and COM objects.

- **HKEY_CURRENT_USER (HKCU):** Stores settings specific to the currently logged-in user.

- **HKEY_LOCAL_MACHINE (HKLM):** Holds settings applicable to all users on the computer.

- **HKEY_USERS (HKU):** Contains user profiles for all users on the system.

- **HKEY_CURRENT_CONFIG (HKCC):** Stores information about the current hardware profile.

How do I access and use the Group Policy Editor?

The **Group Policy Editor** (gpedit.msc) is a tool that allows administrators and advanced users to configure system settings and policies that govern both the operating system and user environments. Use with caution. It's particularly useful for managing security settings, application restrictions, and other administrative configurations.

Availability

- **Windows 11 Editions:** The Group Policy Editor is available in Windows 11 Pro, Enterprise, and Education editions. It is **not** included in the Home edition by default.

Accessing the Group Policy Editor

1. **Open Run Dialog:**

   ☐ Press Win + R to open the Run dialog.

2. **Launch Group Policy Editor:**

   ☐ Type gpedit.msc and press **Enter**.

3. **Alternate Method:**

   ☐ Press Win + X to open the Quick Access Menu.

   ☐ Select **Run**.

   ☐ Type gpedit.msc and press **Enter**.

Navigating the Group Policy Editor Interface

The Group Policy Editor is divided into two main sections:

1. **Computer Configuration:**

   ☐ Contains policies that apply to the entire computer,

regardless of the user logged in.

☐ **Subsections:**

☐ **Policies:** Administrative templates and settings for the computer.

☐ **Windows Settings:** Security settings, scripts, and more.

☐ **Software Settings:** Application management policies.

2. **User Configuration:**

☐ Contains policies that apply to individual users, regardless of which computer they log into.

☐ **Subsections:**

☐ **Policies:** Administrative templates and settings for users.

☐ **Windows Settings:** Security settings, scripts, and more.

☐ **Software Settings:** Application management policies.

How do I Refresh Windows 11 Components?

Sometimes, specific Windows components may become corrupted or misconfigured. **DISM** (Deployment Image Servicing and Management) and **SFC** (System File Checker) are command-line tools that can repair these components.

1. **Open Command Prompt as Administrator:**

   o Press Win + X and select **Windows PowerShell (Admin)** or **Command Prompt (Admin)**.

2. **Run DISM Tool:**

   o Type the following command and press **Enter**:

   ```
   DISM /Online /Cleanup-Image /RestoreHealth
   ```

   o This command scans and repairs the Windows image.

3. **Run SFC Tool:**

o After DISM completes, type the following command and press **Enter**:

```
sfc /scannow
```

o This command scans and repairs corrupted system files.

4. **Restart Your Computer:**

o After both commands finish, restart your computer to apply the repairs.

How do I Calibrate my Monitor?

Calibrating your monitor in Windows 11 ensures accurate color reproduction, brightness, and contrast. Useful for graphic designers, photographers, video editors, and other visual artists need consistent and accurate colors to ensure their work looks the same across devices and in print.

Step 1: Access Display Calibration

1. **Open Settings**:

o Press **Windows + I** to open Settings.

o Navigate to **System > Display**.

2. **Open Color Calibration Tool**:

o Scroll down and click on **Advanced display**.

o Click on **Display adapter properties for Display X** (replace "X" with the monitor number).

o In the dialog box, select to the **Color Management** tab.

o Click **Color Management** and then in the dialog box that pops up, select the **Advanced** tab.

o Under "Display Calibration," click **Calibrate display**. This opens the Display Color Calibration tool.

Step 2: Use the Display Color Calibration Tool

1. **Follow the Instructions**:

o The calibration tool will guide you through steps to adjust:

- **Gamma**: Controls the luminance of colors.

- **Brightness and Contrast**: Ensures the proper display of dark and light areas.

- **Color Balance**: Balances the intensity of red, green, and blue.

2. **Adjust Gamma**:

   o Use the slider to match the example image where circles are just barely visible.

3. **Set Brightness and Contrast**:

   o Use your monitor's physical buttons to adjust these settings. Follow the on-screen guide for optimal levels.

4. **Adjust Color Balance**:

   o Remove any color cast by adjusting sliders for red, green, and blue.

5. **Finish Calibration**:

   o Save the calibration profile.

   o Do the same for other monitors if you have them connected.

Tips for Better Calibration

- Calibrate in a room with consistent lighting.

- Avoid glare or reflections on the screen.

How do I enable Virtualization?

Virtualization in Windows 11 allows you to run multiple operating systems in isolated environments, often used for testing, development, or enhanced security. Before using virtualization features in Windows, ensure that virtualization is enabled in your computer's BIOS or UEFI firmware. These are general guidelines, refer to your system documentation for exact instructions.

1. Restart your PC and enter the BIOS/UEFI settings (usually by pressing Del, F2, or Esc during startup).

2. Look for options like:

   o **Intel VT-x** (Intel systems)

- o **AMD-V** (AMD systems)

- o **SVM Mode** (AMD systems)

3. Enable the relevant virtualization option.

4. Save changes and reboot.

To use virtualization in Windows 11, ensure the relevant features enabled in Windows.

1. Press **Win + R** to open the Run dialog box. Type `appwiz.cpl` then press Enter.

2. Click **Turn Windows features on or off.**

3. Enable the following (as needed):

   - o **Hyper-V** used for creating and managing virtual machines on Windows, supporting various operating systems like Windows and Linux

   - o **Virtual Machine Platform** enables lightweight virtualization features and is essential for running tools like WSL 2.

   - o **Windows Hypervisor Platform** provides an interface for running third-party virtual machine application.

   - o **Windows Subsystem for Linux**: For running Linux distributions.

4. Click **OK** and restart your computer.

How do I Create Virtual Machines with Hyper-V

Hyper-V is a native virtualization solution included in Windows 11 Pro, Enterprise, and Education editions.

Step 1: Open Hyper-V Manager

1. Press Win + S to open the search bar.

2. Type **Hyper-V Manager** and click to open the application.

Step 2: Select Your Computer

1. In the left-hand pane of Hyper-V Manager, locate and select your computer name.

Step 3: Create a New Virtual Machine

Chapter 6: Advanced Settings & Tools

1. In the right-hand **Actions** pane, click **New > Virtual Machine**.

2. The New Virtual Machine Wizard will guide you through the process:

   o **Name the VM**: Enter a descriptive name for the VM (e.g., "Windows 10 Test").

   o **Specify Generation**:

      ▪ Choose **Generation 1** for most operating systems.

      ▪ Choose **Generation 2** for 64-bit OSs requiring UEFI.

   o **Allocate Memory**: Assign RAM for the VM. For modern OSs, at least 4GB (4096MB) is recommended.

   o **Configure Networking**: Select a virtual switch for network connectivity (e.g., Default Switch).

   o **Create a Virtual Hard Disk**: Specify the size (e.g., 50GB for Windows 10/11).

   o **Point to an ISO File**: In the Installation Options, select **Install an operating system from a bootable image file** and browse to the ISO file for the OS you want to install.

Step 4: Start the Virtual Machine

Select the newly created VM from the list in Hyper-V Manager. Click **Start** in the Actions pane.

Right-click the VM and choose **Connect** to open the VM console. Follow the OS installation process as you would on a physical machine.

How do I Create Virtual Machines with VirtualBox?

VirtualBox, developed by Oracle, is an open-source virtualization platform that allows users to run multiple operating systems on a single machine. It is free to use making it a popular choice for both casual users and developers. VirtualBox supports Windows, Linux, macOS, and many others.

Step 1: Download and Install VirtualBox

Go to the following website and download the Windows installer.

`www.virtualbox.org/wiki/Downloads`

Run the installer and follow the prompts, accepting the default options.

Step 2: Create a Virtual Machine

1. Open VirtualBox and click **New** in the toolbar.

2. Fill in the details, click **Next**.

   o **Name**: Name your VM (e.g., "Windows Test").

   o **ISO:** In the ISO Image field, select the installation image for the operating system you're installing.

   o **Type**: Choose the OS type (e.g., Linux, Windows).

   o **Version**: Select the specific version.

   o **Unattended Installation:** Uncheck this option

3. Configure resources:

    o   **Memory (RAM)**: Allocate sufficient memory (e.g., 8GB for most OSs).

    o   **Hard Disk**: Choose **Create a virtual hard disk now** and follow the wizard to specify size and format (e.g., 50GB, VDI format).

4. Start the VM

    o   Click the Start icon.

    o   Run through the OS Installation.

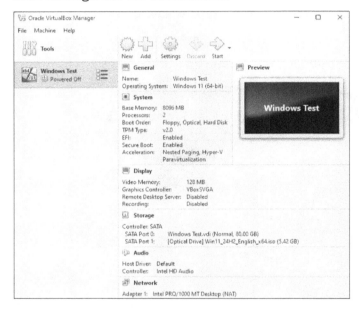

7 Security

How do I protect my PC against malware and viruses?

How do I set up and use Windows Hello?

How do I enable and use BitLocker in Windows 11?

How do I use SmartScreen?

How do I protect myself against Cyber Threats?

Chapter 7: Security

How do I protect my PC against malware and viruses?

Protecting your Windows 11 PC from malware and viruses involves a combination of built-in tools, best practices, and proactive monitoring.

1. Utilize Microsoft Defender Antivirus:

- **Real-Time Protection:**

  o **Enable Real-Time Scanning:**

    - Open **Windows Security** by navigating to Settings > Privacy & Security > Windows Security and clicking **Open Windows Security**.

    - Select **Virus & threat protection**.

    - Ensure that **Real-time protection** is turned **On**.

- **Perform Regular Scans:**

  o **Quick Scan:** Checks the areas most likely to be infected.

  o **Full Scan:** Examines the entire system for threats.

    - **How to Perform a Full Scan:**

      - In **Windows Security**, go to **Virus & threat protection**.

      - Click on **Scan options**.

      - Select **Full scan** and click **Scan now**.

- **Schedule Scans:**

  o **Automate Scans:**

    - Open **Task Scheduler** (Win + R, type taskschd. msc, and press **Enter**).

    - Navigate to **Task Scheduler Library > Microsoft > Windows > Windows Defender**.

    - Configure scheduled scans as per your preference.

2. Keep Your System and Software Updated:

- **Enable Automatic Updates:**

  - Go to Settings > Windows Update.

- Ensure that **Automatic Updates** are enabled to receive the latest security patches.

- **Update Third-Party Software:**

  - Regularly update applications and drivers to patch vulnerabilities that could be exploited by malware.

3. Use Windows Defender Firewall:

- **Ensure Firewall is Active:**

  - Open **Windows Security**.

  - Navigate to **Firewall & network protection**.

  - Verify that the firewall is enabled for all network profiles (Domain, Private, Public).

- **Configure Firewall Settings:**

  - **Block Unauthorized Access:**

    - Create custom rules to allow or block specific applications or ports.

    - Example: Blocking an application from accessing the internet.

4. Practice Safe Browsing and Downloading:

- **Avoid Suspicious Websites:**

  - Refrain from visiting websites known for distributing malware or engaging in phishing.

- **Verify Download Sources:**

  - Download software only from official or reputable sources.

  - Check digital signatures and reviews before installing applications.

- **Use Browser Protections:**

  - Enable **SmartScreen** in Microsoft Edge:

    - Open Edge and go to Settings > Privacy, search, and services.

    - Under **Security**, ensure that **Microsoft Defender SmartScreen** is enabled.

5. Implement Controlled Folder Access:

- **Protect Sensitive Folders:**
    - Open **Windows Security**.
    - Navigate to **Virus & threat protection**.
    - Click on **Manage ransomware protection**.
    - Toggle **Controlled folder access** to **On**.
    - Add important folders (e.g., Documents, Pictures) to the protected list.

6. Enable Network Protection:

- **Prevent Apps from Connecting to Malicious Domains:**
    - Open **Windows Security**.
    - Go to **App & browser control**.
    - Under **Exploit protection**, enable **Network protection**.

7. Use Anti-Malware Tools:

- **Consider Third-Party Solutions:**
    - o While Microsoft Defender is robust, some users may prefer additional layers of protection from reputable third-party antivirus programs like Bitdefender, Norton, or Kaspersky.

8. Educate Yourself and Stay Informed:

- **Stay Updated on Threats:**
    - o Regularly read about new malware threats and security best practices.
    - o Follow trusted security blogs and subscribe to newsletters.

- **Enable User Account Control (UAC):**
    - o Prevent unauthorized changes to your system by ensuring UAC is enabled:
        - Go to Control Panel > User Accounts > Change User Account Control settings.
        - Set the slider to **Always notify** for maximum

protection.

9. Backup Important Data Regularly:

- **Use OneDrive or External Drives:**

  o   Regular backups ensure that you can restore your data in case of a malware attack or system failure.

- **Enable File History:**

  o   Go to Settings > Update & Security > Backup.

  o   Set up **File History** to automatically back up your files.

10. Enable Multi-Factor Authentication (MFA):

- **Add an Extra Layer of Security:**

  o   Use MFA for your Microsoft account and other critical services to prevent unauthorized access even if your password is compromised.

How do I set up and use Windows Hello?

Windows Hello is a biometric authentication system in Windows 11 that provides a secure and convenient way to sign into your device using facial recognition, fingerprint scanning, or a PIN.

1. Ensure Hardware Compatibility:

- **Facial Recognition:**

  o   Requires a compatible infrared (IR) camera or a Windows Hello-compatible camera.

- **Fingerprint Scanning:**

  o   Requires a fingerprint reader.

- **PIN:**

  o   Available on all Windows 11 devices.

2. Setting Up Windows Hello:

A. Setting Up Facial Recognition:

- **Open Settings:**

  o   Press Win + I to open **Settings**.

Chapter 7: Security

- **Navigate to Accounts:**

    o Go to Accounts > Sign-in options.

- **Select Windows Hello Face:**

    o Under **Manage how you sign in to your device**, click on **Windows Hello Face**.

- **Click on Set Up:**

    o Follow the on-screen instructions to position your face within the camera frame.

- **Complete Enrollment:**

    o After successful recognition, you can add a backup PIN if prompted.

B. Setting Up Fingerprint Scanning:

- **Open Settings:**

    o Press Win + I to open **Settings**.

- **Navigate to Accounts:**

    o Go to Accounts > Sign-in options.

- **Select Windows Hello Fingerprint:**

    o Click on **Windows Hello Fingerprint**.

- **Click on Set Up:**

    o Follow the on-screen prompts to scan your fingerprint using the fingerprint reader.

- **Add Additional Fingers (Optional):**

    o You can add multiple fingerprints for different fingers.

C. Setting Up a PIN:

- **Open Settings:**

    o Press Win + I to open **Settings**.

- **Navigate to Accounts:**

    o Go to Accounts > Sign-in options.

- **Select PIN:**

o   Click on **Windows Hello PIN**.

• **Click on Add:**

  o   Enter your Microsoft account password for verification.

• **Create a PIN:**

  o   Enter a secure PIN and confirm it. Optionally, you can enable the **PIN requirements** for added security.

3. Managing Windows Hello Settings:

• **Change or Remove Authentication Methods:**

  o   In Settings > Accounts > Sign-in options, you can modify or remove existing Windows Hello methods.

• **Set Up Additional Authentication Methods:**

  o   You can use multiple methods (e.g., facial recognition and PIN) for added flexibility and security.

How do I enable and use BitLocker in Windows 11?

BitLocker is a full-disk encryption feature in Windows 11 that protects your data by encrypting your entire drive. Enabling BitLocker ensures that your data remains secure, even if your device is lost or stolen.

Check Hardware Requirements:

• **Trusted Platform Module (TPM) 2.0:**

  o   BitLocker requires TPM 2.0 for secure key storage.

  o   **Verify TPM Presence:**

    •   Press Win + R, type tpm.msc, and press **Enter**.

    •   Ensure that **TPM is ready for use** and that the **Specification Version** is 2.0.

• **Administrator Privileges:**

  o   You must be logged in with an account that has administrative rights to enable BitLocker.

Enabling BitLocker:

Open Control Panel:

  o   Press Win + R, type control, and press **Enter**.

177

1. **Navigate to BitLocker Drive Encryption:**

    o   Go to System and Security > BitLocker Drive Encryption.

2. **Turn On BitLocker:**

    o   Click **Turn on BitLocker** next to the drive you wish to encrypt (typically the C: drive).

3. **Choose Authentication Method:**

    o   **TPM Only:** Uses TPM for encryption without requiring a USB key.

    o   **TPM with PIN:** Adds an additional layer by requiring a PIN during startup.

    o   **TPM with USB Key:** Requires a USB flash drive containing the encryption key during startup.

    o   **Choose as per your security needs** and click **Next**.

4. **Backup Your Recovery Key:**

    o   **Options:**

        ▪   Save to your Microsoft account.

        ▪   Save to a USB flash drive.

        ▪   Save to a file (preferably stored securely offline).

        ▪   Print the recovery key.

    o   **Recommendation:** Save the recovery key to a secure location separate from your device.

5. **Choose Encryption Mode:**

    o   **New Encryption Mode (XTS-AES):** Recommended for fixed drives.

    o   **Compatible Mode (AES-CBC):** Suitable if you plan to move the drive between different versions of Windows.

6. **Start Encryption:**

    o   Click **Start Encrypting** to begin the encryption process.

    o   **Note:** Encryption time varies based on drive size and system performance.

Managing BitLocker:

Pausing BitLocker:

- **When Needed:**

  o Temporarily disable BitLocker, for example, during system updates or hardware changes.

1. **Open Control Panel:**

   o Navigate to System and Security > BitLocker Drive Encryption.

2. **Pause Protection:**

   o Click **Suspend protection** next to the encrypted drive.

   o Confirm the action when prompted.

Resuming BitLocker:

1. **Open Control Panel:**

   o Navigate to System and Security > BitLocker Drive Encryption.

2. **Resume Protection:**

   o Click **Resume protection** next to the encrypted drive.

Changing BitLocker Settings:

- **Modify Authentication Methods:**

  o Update PINs or passwords used for BitLocker authentication.

- **Change Encryption Method:**

  o Transition between encryption modes if necessary via the **Manage BitLocker** options.

Decrypting a Drive:

1. **Open Control Panel:**

   o Navigate to System and Security > BitLocker Drive Encryption.

2. **Turn Off BitLocker:**

   o Click **Turn off BitLocker** next to the encrypted

drive.

o Confirm the action and follow the prompts to decrypt the drive.

How do I use SmartScreen?

SmartScreen is a security feature in Windows 11 designed to protect your PC from malicious websites, phishing attempts, and potentially harmful downloads.

Ensure SmartScreen is Enabled

1. Open **Settings**:

   o Press Win + I to open the Settings app.

2. Navigate to **Privacy & Security** > **Windows Security**.

3. Click **App & Browser Control**.

4. In the **Reputation-based protection** section, click **Reputation-based protection settings**.

5. Ensure the following toggles are enabled:

   o **Check apps and files**: Warns you about potentially dangerous files.

   o **SmartScreen for Microsoft Edge**: Blocks malicious websites and phishing attempts when using Edge.

   o **SmartScreen for Microsoft Store apps**: Ensures apps from the Microsoft Store are safe.

Use SmartScreen While Browsing (Microsoft Edge)

▢ When visiting websites, SmartScreen works in the background to analyze URLs. If you try to visit a suspicious or known malicious site, you'll see a warning screen.

▢ Options on the warning screen:

   o **Go back**: Safely exit the website.

   o **Report this site**: Send feedback to Microsoft if you believe the site is wrongly flagged.

   o **Ignore and proceed**: Only do this if you're absolutely sure the site is safe.

Use SmartScreen for Downloads

☐ When downloading files, SmartScreen will scan the file and warn you if it detects anything suspicious.

☐ You'll see options to:

  o **Delete the file**: If it's deemed unsafe.

  o **Keep the file**: Only if you are confident it's secure.

Customize SmartScreen Notifications

☐ You can control how aggressive SmartScreen is with warnings:

  1. Go to **Reputation-based protection settings**.

  2. Choose to turn off certain features or adjust settings for apps, files, or Edge.

Review Blocked Content

☐ If SmartScreen blocks a download or site you need to access:

  1. Check the details on the warning screen.

  2. Only proceed if you're confident the content is safe.

Manage SmartScreen for Microsoft Store Apps

☐ This ensures that apps installed from the Store are verified and free from malware.

☐ You can enable or disable this setting in the **Reputation-based protection settings**.

Benefits of Using SmartScreen

☐ Blocks known phishing and malware sites.

☐ Warns you about suspicious apps and downloads.

☐ Protects your sensitive data while browsing.

How do I protect myself against Cyber Threats?

In today's digital age, cyber threats are a constant and evolving challenge. With this in mind Windows 11 includes various security features to help protect your data and privacy. However, no system is entirely immune, and understanding common cyber threats is essential for staying safe.

Chapter 7: Security

Phishing Attacks

Phishing tricks users into revealing sensitive information (e.g., passwords, financial details) via fake emails, websites, or messages that appear legitimate. These come from various sources such as:

- Emails from fake companies (e.g., "Your bank account is locked").
- SMS messages (smishing) pretending to be package delivery updates or urgent alerts.
- Fake websites mimicking login pages for services like Microsoft, Google, or social media.
- Social media direct messages (e.g., "Check out this link").

You can help protect yourself against these threats using the following options:

1. **Enable Microsoft Defender SmartScreen**: Automatically blocks phishing websites and untrusted downloads.
2. **Verify URLs**: Hover over links in emails and texts to check the actual URL before clicking. Ensure it starts with "https://" and matches the official website.
3. **Avoid Clicking on Attachments**: Do not open unexpected attachments or links, especially from unknown senders.
4. **Use Anti-Phishing Tools**: Many browsers and security programs (like Microsoft Defender) include anti-phishing filters.
5. **Enable Multi-Factor Authentication (MFA)**: Even if attackers obtain your password, MFA adds a second layer of defense.
6. **Educate Yourself and Employees**: Training to recognize phishing attempts significantly reduces risks.

Malware

Malware refers to malicious software like viruses, worms, trojans, spyware, and adware designed to harm, steal, or disrupt your system. These come from various sources such as:

- Malicious email attachments (e.g., fake invoices or resumes).
- Infected websites or ads.
- Free or pirated software downloads from untrusted sources.
- USB drives or external storage infected with malware.

You can help protect yourself against these threats using the following options:

1. **Keep Software Updated**: Install updates for Windows, browsers, and all applications regularly to patch vulnerabilities.

2. **Enable Windows Defender Antivirus**: Provides real-time protection against malware threats.

3. **Avoid Downloads from Untrusted Sources**: Only download software from official or verified websites.

4. **Scan External Devices**: Use antivirus software to scan USB drives or external devices before opening files.

5. **Use Sandboxing or Virtual Machines**: Test suspicious software in isolated environments like Windows Sandbox.

Ransomware

Ransomware encrypts your files and demands payment to restore access. These come from various sources such as:

- Email attachments with malicious scripts.

- Fake/Infected websites or downloads.

You can help protect yourself against these threats using the following options:

1. **Enable Controlled Folder Access**: In Windows Security, restrict access to important files from unauthorized apps.

2. **Regular Backups**: Store backups on external drives or cloud storage to recover files without paying the ransom.

3. **Avoid Clicking on Unknown Links**: Don't download files or click links from unsolicited emails.

4. **Keep Security Software Updated**: Ensure your antivirus and firewall are up to date.

5. **Use Application Whitelisting**: Limit which programs can execute on your system.

6. **Don't pay the ransom:** This usually doesn't resolve the problem or decrypt your files.

Zero-Day Vulnerabilities

Exploits targeting undiscovered or unpatched vulnerabilities in software.

These come from various sources such as:

- Browsers, plugins (e.g., Flash, Java), and unpatched software.

- Malicious email attachments or links.

You can help protect yourself against these threats using the following options:

1. **Regular Updates**: Always update Windows and software to patch vulnerabilities.

2. **Use Exploit Mitigation Tools**: Features like Windows Defender Exploit Guard help mitigate the risk of exploits.

3. **Isolate Untrusted Applications**: Use Windows Sandbox or a virtual machine to open suspicious files or software.

4. **Limit Admin Privileges**: Use a standard user account for daily tasks.

Man-in-the-Middle (MITM) Attacks

Attackers intercept communications between two parties to steal or manipulate data. These come from various sources such as:

- Unsecured public Wi-Fi networks.

- Rogue Wi-Fi hotspots set up by attackers.

- Compromised routers with outdated firmware.

You can help protect yourself against these threats using the following options:

1. **Avoid Public Wi-Fi**: Use a Virtual Private Network (VPN) for secure connections.

2. **Use HTTPS**: Ensure websites use HTTPS for encrypted communication.

3. **Secure Your Router**: Change default credentials, enable WPA3 encryption, and keep firmware updated.

4. **Enable Windows Firewall**: Blocks unauthorized network activity.

Social Engineering

Manipulation tactics used to trick users into revealing information or bypassing security protocols.

These come from various sources such as:

- Fake phone calls (e.g., "This is Microsoft support").

- Impersonation of colleagues or authority figures via email or phone.

- Urgent messages creating fear (e.g., "Your account will be deleted in 24 hours").

You can help protect yourself against these threats using the following options:

1. **Verify Identities**: Always confirm requests for sensitive information via a trusted channel.

2. **Educate Yourself and Others**: Awareness of common social engineering tactics reduces risks.

3. **Be Skeptical of Urgent Requests**: Fraudsters often create a sense of urgency.

4. **Limit Shared Information**: Avoid oversharing personal details online.

Credential Theft

Attackers steal login credentials via phishing, malware, or brute-force attacks. These come from various sources such as:

- Keyloggers or spyware.

- Phishing emails and fake login pages.

- Unencrypted network traffic on public Wi-Fi.

You can help protect yourself against these threats using the following options:

1. **Enable Multi-Factor Authentication (MFA)**: Prevents unauthorized access even if passwords are compromised.

2. **Use a Password Manager**: Creates and stores strong, unique passwords for each account.

3. **Monitor Login Activity**: Check account activity for unauthorized logins.

4. **Use Windows Credential Guard**: Protects login credentials in memory.

Video Resources

To help you understand the procedures and concepts explored in this book, we have developed some video resources and app demos for you to use, as you work through the book.

As well as the video resources, you'll also find some downloadable files and samples for exercises that appear in the book.

To find the resources, open your web browser and navigate to the following website

```
elluminetpress.com/win-11/
```

Do not use a search engine, type the website into the address field at the top of the browser window.

Using the Videos

Type the website url into the address bar at the top of your browser.

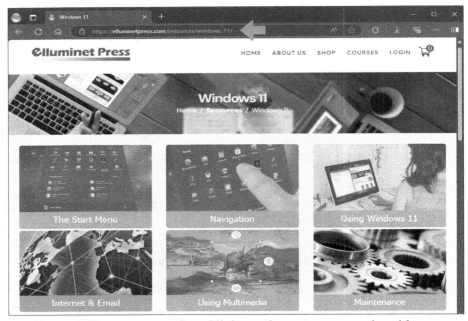

You'll see different categories. Click on these to access the videos.

When you open the link to the video resources, you'll see a thumbnail list at the bottom.

Click on the thumbnail for the particular video you want to watch. Most videos are between 40 and 90 seconds outlining the procedure, others are a bit longer.

When the video is playing, hover your mouse over the video and you'll see some controls...

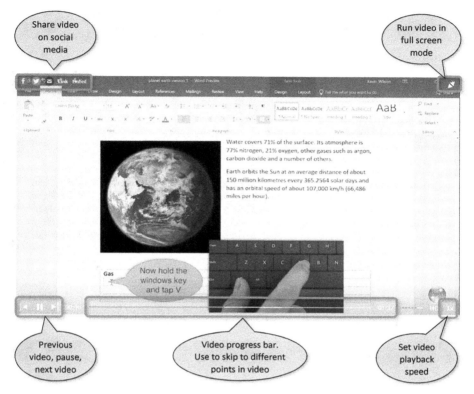

Here, you can share the video on social media, make it full screen. You can also play/pause the video, jump to a particular part of the video using the progress bar and set the playback speed.

Other Resources

You'll also find cheat sheets, short-cuts, updates, tips and frequently asked questions.

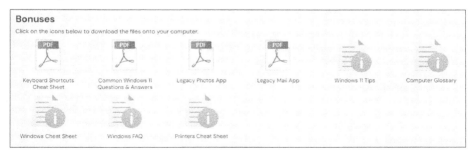

Video Resources

You'll also find a tips section. Here, we'll keep you up to date with the latest tips and tricks to help you get the most out of Windows 11.

Finally, you'll find a glossary of computing terms.

You can find the index here:

www.elluminetpress.com/glossary

This is integrated into the resources section.

Index

Index

Index

Index

SOMETHING
NOT COVERED?

We want to create the best possible resources to help you learn and get things done, so if we've missed anything out, then please get in touch using the links below and let us know. Thanks.

 office@elluminetpress.com

 elluminetpress.com/feedback

www.ingramcontent.com/pod-product-compliance
Lightning Source LLC
Chambersburg PA
CBHW071150050326
40689CB00011B/2048